STROUD

A Town Changed by Community Action

Camilla Hale
Dominique Shead

Stroud Preservation Trust

Dedication

This book is dedicated to Richard Feilden and Clare Toy, who worked with and inspired so many different projects and groups.

Also, of course, we dedicate this book to the hundreds of people that have made Stroud a wonderful town to live in, and to all those who in the future will continue to campaign and work for our town.

1st Edition published December 2013
2nd Edition published January 2014
Published by:
Stroud Preservation Trust (est. 1982)
Registered Office:
6 Castle Villas
Stroud
Glos GL5 2HP

Email: info@stroudpreservationtrust.org.uk
Charity Number 284255
Company Number 1608981
www.stroudpreservationtrust.org.uk/
www.facebook.com/stroudcommunityaction

ISBN 978-1-906662-13-4

Designed by Paul Welch, www.welchpix.co.uk
Printed and bound by in the UK by StroudPrint, www.stroudprint.co.uk

Contents

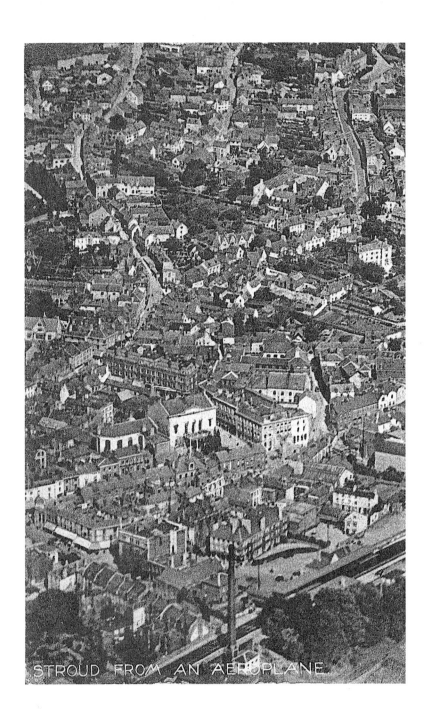

STROUD FROM AN AEROPLANE

Introduction

STROUD – A TOWN CHANGED BY COMMUNITY ACTION looks at ten projects covering the last forty years (from 1975). These projects sprung up for different reasons – economic, social, environmental, historic preservation – but underlying all of them was a commitment to community, to being part of a democratic process, to shaping the town that we live in.

The book has been written because Stroud Preservation Trust celebrated its 30th birthday in 2012 and in researching the history and actions of the Trust there was an obvious debt to previous successful campaigns and a link and connection to many other projects over the years. We wanted to acknowledge some of the extraordinary community work that has made such a difference to the town, and try to answer questions like: what is the catalyst for action, how do organisations develop, how do they keep going?

At the back of the book is an ever-growing list of community projects. Organisations and initiatives, actions and campaigns will inevitably be missing from this list but it is exciting to see how readily people get involved and work for change. Ten of those projects were chosen for this book, but there are many more to write about!

All ten projects have faced tremendous challenges, but they started with a fierce sense of belief in taking action. Shire Training Workshops pioneered employment and work for young people in Gloucestershire in the late '70s. Stroud Preservation Trust and Stroud Valleys Project were set up to influence the built and natural environment. The Community Planning Conference involved thousands of people deciding on the priorities for the town. Economic action at the Old Convent and the Farmers' Market have built new business communities; planning campaigns say 'no' and help shape development decisions; and the Museum in the Park holds our social history for the future.

Many of these projects were inspired by the tremendous successes of the Ring Road and High Street campaigns in stopping the demolition of parts of Stroud. These two major events in the '70s and early '80s, along with the Stratford Park Trees and Hill Paul campaigns, have been covered in more detail in articles in Tamsin Treverton Jones's book, *Memories of Stroud*. Their role cannot be underestimated and the first two campaigns are acknowledged in the Stroud Preservation Trust chapter. However, for this book we wanted to look at projects that have not been written about to date.

We interviewed 30 people and compiled their many hours of testimony into a very condensed version – to those involved I hope this can be a real stimulus to collate and archive your wonderful records and to write books about your own remarkable organisations. Many people involved in these campaigns were new-comers to Stroud – attracted to the town because 'they liked its character and feeling, its industrial and creative heritage, its alternative institutions, low-priced housing and surrounding landscape. They saw the town for its potential and the surrounding countryside for its real beauty... many newcomers felt that local people did not value what they had and were still keen on the 'demolish and redevelop' post-war mentality'.[1]

Roger Franklin says that 'Stroud was already known for its strong bohemian vibe and history of alternative politics'[3] and new protesters and campaigners felt sup-ported by this history – the Whiteway Colony, the growing Steiner community, and a sense of the mill protests from the 19th century.

'Ordinary people should be able to influence what happens in the community,' says Mike Goodenough [2] – such a simple statement and such a strong motiva-tion for so many. Over the past decades we have realised that some in the com-munity are the resource, the skilled and the visionary and that if we don't get on with an idea of change, who will? Hence the Community Planning logo – Up2Us.

Many of the early campaigns were very strongly against the District Council, fuelled by a real antagonism at the lack of community involvement. In the book this focus is not so strong; the organisations that developed have worked closely with the Council. There have been setbacks, but essentially the Council came on board more and more through the '80s and '90s alongside community action. Planning campaigns themselves have changed from being 'against' to 'working with'. Often community groups can focus much more clearly on issues than councils can, and spend hundreds of hours amassing evidence to support a council's position in appeals – Slad Valleys Action Group (both campaigns) have taken this line by setting themselves up as an information point for SDC.

The other side of campaigning is publicity and endless imaginative approaches have been taken – furry godfathers, a three wishes campaign, a whiteboard of signatures, songs and poetry. And many of the campaigns, actions and local groups have been 100 per cent backed by the local press. Articles and letters in the *Stroud News and Journal*, *The Citizen* and later *Stroud Life* have fuelled both sides of various arguments and been an essential forum for debate.

Campaigns, protests, community action and local businesses add to the mix of Stroud and build on each other. Each campaign and each successful venture grows success, revival and investment in the town. This accumulated critical mass is vital; there are people of many generations now with skills in start-ups, funding, successful publicity, appeals, legal experience. The District Council and Town Councils are made up of many of these activists, who themselves bring knowledge and struggle to the political table. Community consultation is assumed (if not always done) and people feel far more confident now than they did to say 'No No No'. Or 'Yes yes yes'! [4]

Our dedication is to the many hundreds of people involved in shaping Stroud over the decades into a vibrant town. We also dedicate this book to the many hundreds more who will continue this work and ride on the shoulders of those who have realised that strong community action has great value and can really engender change.

1.Nigel Paterson, 'The Vernacular Architecture and Buildings of Stroud and Chalford' (Oxford, 2006)
2.Tamsin Treverton Jones, 'Memories of Stroud' (Stroud 2005)
3.Rebecca Price, 'A Study into Local Protest in Stroud, 1975–present' (2012)
4.Clare Toy, 'The Plotter of Gloucester' (Stroud 1976). 'The people of Stroud stood up and said No, No, No!'

Below: Dr Fosters Mad Hatter Tea Party at the Old Convent, early '80s
Bottom: Aerial view of the buildings

1

The 1970s

The Old Convent
1976

'The early days at the Old Convent had the feel of a co-operative venture, with a degree of democracy and involvement for those of us in the building – definitely not a standard landlord/tenant relationship. People and ideas came and went fast, aided by a considerable feeling of community and support from all those involved, and the lines between work and the rest of life were pleasantly blurred. I guess the early interest in the building was very much one of re-using an otherwise redundant and unloved building, which fortunately has at last become fashionable. Keith, Bea and Jens were central to the community, particularly their kitchen, until the advent of the café in various locations.'

Jonathan Nunn, osteopath & tenant in the Old Convent for the last 20 years.

THE OLD CONVENT IS A MAGNIFICENT building, Grade II listed, tucked in behind the Catholic church on Beeches Green and behind high yew hedges that face the Merrywalks shopping centre. The building was designed by Benjamin Bucknell, a vigorous and inventive architect inspired by medieval building techniques. He was also the architect of the now more famous Woodchester Mansion. Built in 1862, the Convent of St Roses was lived in by Dominican sisters, running a school and then later establishing St Roses school for children with disabilities. The Catholic church of the Immaculate Conception had its first mass in 1852. Both were part of a mid 19th-century dynamic Catholic revival in the Stroud Valleys.

By the early 1970s education provision had changed with the new Rosary School being built and St Peter's secondary school in Gloucester. The nuns (by the end only ten of them) had moved out and the building was empty. Stroud District Council refused to allow some of the building to be knocked down to widen access to the school in 1978 and its new role gradually emerged. This role was to be a welcoming hub, a series of spaces of all sizes for a huge variety of businesses and organisations and individual practitioners.

During the late '60s Keith and Bea Morgan had moved from Bournemouth, where Keith was studying architecture, to London into a huge squat where they met many people who would remain friends for life. Keith worked at the Environmental Consulting Office in Great Newport Street and it was there that he met Peter Waller, who was the project co-ordinator. In the early '70s Peter Waller moved to Stroud and he then tempted Keith and Bea to come down and look at a building he was interested in. 'We immediately thought of a working community,' says Keith, 'because the eco practice in London had been instrumental in setting up Clerkenwell workshops, a multi mix use renovating redundant industrial buildings for small businesses including organisations like Spare Rib. Keith and Bea spent the weekend with Peter and talked about a rural working community here based on what Peter had seen locally, people he'd met, the interest raised. 'We agreed we'd do it and move to Stroud with our small son Jens.'

Keith continues: 'The building was unused; it had been empty since 1972. The sisters had already decamped to a special place down the road, so the Convent had been empty for four years and there was a lot of damage to it. It hadn't been maintained and the sisters were desperate because their architects had tried change of use from just about everything they could think of. There was a lot of opposition from the priest at the church.

'We had completely clandestine negotiations with the English Dominican Congregation, which took about 18 months to put in place, negotiating a three-year rent-free period at least against a schedule of works to be completed. When it was all signed up, the church was incandescent that they'd done this and on the afternoon we arrived here with all our stuff in a 5-ton truck, we were unloading in the courtyard and the priest marched up to me and he said, "I'll have you out of here in three months," and turned on his heel and flapped off. So it was a bit worrying, the intent of the man, what was he going to do? As

Entrance to the Old Convent

the years went by I never warmed to him, but we did speak before he left his post and he did confide that he wanted the Convent pulled down so people from Stroud could see his church without the Convent being in the way.'

There was a good deal of opposition towards the whole venture – uncertainty as to who these newcomers were, what they were doing at the Convent with no leaders despite the fact that this was a large building that was empty and falling into disrepair near the centre of Stroud. There was very little regeneration during the '70s; this was a time when the ring road and High Street were being fought for. The Old Convent was a trendsetter for Stroud.

'We sort of settled in and gradually started bringing people into the building rent free, so there was no money,' continues Keith. 'When we did start charging rents it all went on getting the electricity on. There were perhaps a dozen sockets in the whole building, so it needed complete rewiring. There was water coming in and we did it on a shoestring really. We used a lot of reclaimed material, even reclaimed electrical gear, stuff that was scrounged or from reclamation yards. Luckily we had known Steve Tomlin in London and he was down here as well running his reclamation yard – very useful. As the money came in from the spaces it would go straight into the building. We hit our three-year target: the schedule of repairs was completed and by then the building was pretty much full.

'All through these years Peter was doing the planning negotiations,' continues Keith, 'and that must have taken three or four years because it was an animal that the planners didn't know which cage to put in. We were living here, working here, without any planning permission for about four years until it was finally resolved, so that was quite hairy as well because again we had a lot of opposition, opposition all down the line.

'We took a lease on half the building at first and once that was filled we negotiated a lease on the rest of it as well. It was done in two stages, phase 1 and phase 2. We were based in the building and did all the administration, so we were learning new tricks, doing the books, handling all the agencies involved, creating a business basically and all that goes with it. Plus having a lot of fun and having people here who helped out, like Tim Harrison who was in a joinery workshop here and put a lot of work in doing floors. After three years all the scheduled works had been completed and Peter and I were able to buy the building.

'We had some great parties in those early years,' recalls Keith. 'People really wanted to be here because it was a wonderful building. There was a very flexible, and still is, agreement between who is here and the management – a 30-day licence – and so nobody was roped into a lease or anything which was constrictive, just a 30-day agreement, pay the money at the end of the month and get another month. It's always been like that, even with the businesses here now. Of course that made problems with the banks. They said, well technically, in 30 days the place could be empty so we're not going to lend you any money, but we took all that in our stride. I felt that we were a small business as well – I can remember saying to people, your business is our business really, and we sought no grants and none was offered. So it was a real self-help process from beginning to end.

'After a year or two we set a café down at the end, in what was the refectory,' he says. 'It's a beautiful room with a beautiful floor and with long low arches.' There wasn't any other café of that kind in town then and the Convent café was very much a community café, with people doing shifts.

'I think any place where people come together who have an independent bond and a certain enthusiasm for the alternative – wherever that happens it's going to be a good feeling, always. People were here and being seen to be at the edges of conformity – not necessarily non-conformed, but questioning everything. The possibilities were very much evident in the late '60s early '70s: new ways of doing things, new ways of dressing, new ways of talking, new ways of making money. So yes, wherever people recognise other kindred spirits, I think it's going to burst out, and Stroud seems to have a good number of such people. For the many people that didn't know that the Convent was here it didn't really matter to them, but it did matter to us and the people who

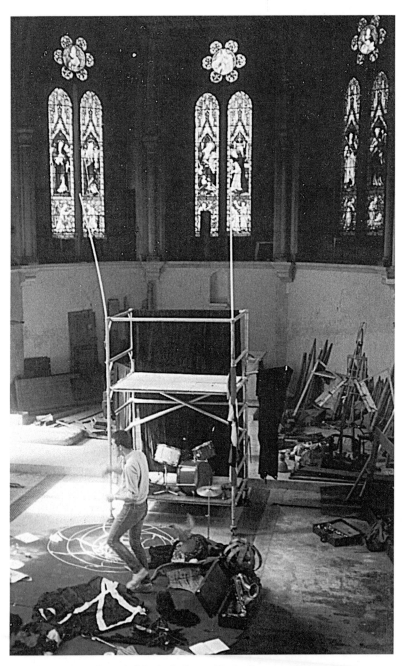

The old chapel in use for set-building by Dr Fosters Theatre Company, 1991

wanted to be here. We created something that was very rewarding for everybody. At the same time we were able to continue on that original schedule of repairs and works and spent money profitably on repairs to the building.'

During the early '80s the Convent was operating at its best. It was full. A new access road was built from Beeches Green Health Centre, which meant that the road along the side of the church was no longer needed. And in 1986 Peter and Keith oversaw the grubbing up of the orchard that went down to Merrywalks and installed a 30-place car park. David Felce, the fish man, turned all the apples into cider and a green place was lost to Stroud.

However, all looked good then, and the Convent really functioned well.

There were changes in the air – more and more mill sites came on line with small start-up units; the community café culture went across the road to Shire Training Workshops and mainstream café culture started at Mills with the development of Withy's Yard. A building like the Convent requires money all the time and Peter and Keith borrowed heavily for improvements like the Chapel roof.

Keith takes up the story: 'What happened? Well, we diversified, which was a mistake. We purchased a business in the belief that it would generate a bit of cash, which it did but not as much as we were anticipating. Stick with what you know is obviously the answer with hindsight. Yes, in '92 we borrowed and of course in '92 came the recession, the second oil recession, so we struggled to hold on to a lot of the tenants. We had saddled ourselves with this big debt, a part of which was supposed to be going to a Chapel development as well and all our business plan forecasts came to nothing. We were stuck. We kept going for about two or three years with the agreement of the principal lender, waiting for the upturn, but it didn't happen for us so we lost it in 1994. I talked to lots of people about reinvesting in the building but in the end Tim Wiltshire and Andrew Ward bought it.

'They asked me if I would stay on and do everything that had been done before really, and so I obviously agreed to that. It was sold to them in '95. Not much actually changed for the Convent, we still had the business centre, I was still here and yes we were still working, but the years had passed and because there is just so much diversity of lettable space in Stroud and around Stroud, anybody who comes here is also probably looking at three or four other places where they can also have a base and office, so it's a lot more competitive.

'Bit by bit we found we were losing ground and we weren't attracting people quite so readily as before, and well yes, at present there's very, very low occupancy. In some ways it's come full circle after 35 years, with not much happening in the building.'

What is the future for a building like this? Perhaps some residential units would bring money into the building. The Convent has some wonderful attributes, it is beautifully built, it is full of different attractive spaces and is a landmark building for Stroud. It also has great cisterns to catch roof water – potential for a full recycled water system. But it is huge, cold, and mere day-to-day maintenance soaks up major capital.

One of the changes that Keith has seen over the years is a move away from small businesses making actual things to more screen-based work. Some of the first tenants are still working there and they have great affection for the place. It has housed textile designers, joiners, computer programmers, accountants, Dr Fosters Theatre Company, healers, osteopaths, secretarial services, graphic designers, chiropractors and artists. The Chapel, now used as a studio space for sculptor Simon Packard, was the place used to prepare the huge sets for the Stroud Community Play in 1991 – no other empty space in Stroud could offer such fantastic size.

'In the end,' says Keith, 'this always has been a fairly insular operation. It always amazed me that beyond the yew hedge people had no idea what we'd done to the Convent, because we didn't really publicise; we seldom had any open weekends, so it's always been a slight mystery about what happens here. Although it's in the middle of the town it seems to almost be a backwater. We were very happy for it to be like that initially because I was aware there were many factions and cliques and allegiances and we never really got involved in that. We had this project to consider and make work, and yes, we didn't really make any strong connections with anybody else. But I am still here and it has been my life now for over 30 years, and it is still a truly wonderful building.'

Interviewee: *Keith Morgan*

Above: The courtyard of the Old Convent.
Left: Promotional postcard for the Stroud Community Play, set built at the Old Convent by Dr Fosters

▲ **Please help us: Mary Lettington and Patrick Mansfield of the Painswick Inn Project outside the pub, for which they have ambitious plans.** (PN-93-62)

Councillors had asked their officers to come up

levels will drop even further.

Urgent appeal launched to give old pub a new lease of life

● A base for the Stroud 'Tools for Self

2 | Shire Training Workshops (OPENhouse) – 1977

The 1970s

'There are an awful lot of people who can't wait until they are 16 to find a safe place to live, so where are they going to go? We've got a lot of work to do with regard to the homeless agenda. We need to look at the ways in which we can be supporting and campaigning for our homeless young people and looking to support those young people. They may never be able to afford to live on their own, so supporting them to be able to live in shared accommodation is the most effective way.'

Claire Mould, Chief Executive OPENhouse

SHIRE TRAINING WORKSHOPS evolved from a deep concern at the end of the 1970s about young people, their high unemployment levels and a society that seemed not to be interested in investing in them and their future. Thirty-six years later – high youth unemployment, homelessness and poverty still persist. The work of Shire Training Workshops has continued until now and looks to be needed well into the future. Over the three and a half decades the project has changed its name several times – Shire Training Workshops, The Painswick Inn Project, The Five Valleys Foyer and currently OPENhouse. This chapter charts the history of the organisation and stays predominantly with the Shire Training Workshops name until the trading name changed to its current form of OPENhouse.

Tom Bermingham starts the story: 'I came to Stroud almost by accident in 1975. I was at Emerson College in Sussex [a college based on the Rudolf Steiner science of the spirit – anthroposophy] and we wanted our children to go to a Steiner school. I put an advert in the *Ecologist* magazine and Ulla and

Ralph Talbot sent us a message, which said that they had a house in Bisley Road. I got a job at Paradise House and worked there for two years. I met Richard Feilden there (his parents lived next door) and as an architect he made quite a difference to Stroud over the years.'

Tom was increasingly concerned about young people and their struggles at this time of 'winters of discontent'. He didn't feel comfortable working for an institution: 'I'd always been left-wing, socialist, anarchist; I'd lived in communes, I was certainly anti-capitalist. So I was very inspired by the ideas which seemed to me a bridge between the spiritual world and social world. I had been studying Steiner's *Threefold Social Order* and I was really aware of his comment about anthroposophy going round and round in ever decreasing bourgeois circles, that it needed to find its place on the street if it was going to work.'

A conversation Tom had with Martin Large crystallised these ideas. And a further 'powerful discussion about anthroposophy and what was needed in the social challenge of the time, including a training programme' involved George Perry in his craft shop, Aurora, on Gloucester Street. Martin Large was the catalyst for action – he had met Tom when at Sussex University and George when they were both teaching at the Steiner school in Bristol.

Martin Large was not part of the working team but he continuously supported the project. He had persuaded a group of consultants to let Tom work in their offices in Gloucester and for a while the project may have taken off in Gloucester. However, the empty Milwards-owned shop on the High Street in Stroud became available shortly after these inspiring conversations and it became possible to demonstrate, in a non-dogmatic way, the principles of anthroposophy directly on the High Street.

Tom managed to negotiate the first Youth Opportunity Programme (YOP) in the county and this enabled initial funding for a project manager, a part-time bookkeeper and two project supervisors to work with young people. Early in 1979 the core group to initiate the project came together and Shire Training

Workshops Ltd was formed with five Directors: Tom Bermingham, George Perry, Helen Tank, Patrick Mansfield and Jan Beaumont. Broadly the roles they took on were: Tom – Project Manager; Helen – Catering Supervisor; Patrick –Building Supervisor; George – Social and Life Skills Tutor and bookkeeper, and Jan – Company Secretary and fundraiser.

Helen Tank was trained in working with young people in care and interested in the challenge of setting up a community café with young people. Patrick had been living in Bath working on the building conversion of Richard Feilden's house. He had met Richard's wife while studying at Bath University where his dissertation had been on 'The Implications of Steiner's Threefold Social Order for Education'. One day Richard said: 'You should go and talk to Tom in Stroud. He's starting a very exciting project.'

George: 'We all went intentionally unemployed in order to get six months' funding. We became a group of co-workers and had regular meetings to think through what we believed in and what we were doing. We were idealistic, in our late 20s and early 30s and we started a café – Starters.'

In early February 1979 the keys to 57 High Street were obtained and the first board meeting of Shire Training Workshops Ltd was held in candlelight. The next was more congenial as a gas heater had been obtained and the desire to re-convene in the Wimpy Bar across the road was not so strong.

Somehow the group had raised some money but, George continues, 'we had moved into a building, just about put down a peppercorn rent for six months, no security. Friends said, "You must be mad! It's going to take you three months to do it up! And then you've got to open it and then in three months you could be chucked out. Why on earth are you doing this?" Then it was essential to start attracting young people.'

Friends and volunteers came to help the café get ready often late into the night. A telling comment from one of the first volunteers on seeing all this activity was, 'I bet no one comes in when we open tomorrow, I bet no one comes in, I bet if they do they'll all be hippies like you lot!'

features

At noon every seat is already taken : solicitors, housewives, teenagers, businessmen, people from every quarter cram into Starter's Café for the liveliest lunch hour in town.

In the mornings or afternoons you can sit there and play chess for as long as you like, or have a free read of the daily papers. Almost every evening something different is on : a teenage party, a play, a concert, a puppet show, a film on Lebo-yer's birth method, or Alan Ginsberg and friends, who stopped off to infuse a bit of New York into an already extraordinary poetry evening.

Stroud, Glos., has never known anything like it. In just a few months this small Cotswold town has been galvanized into a thriving little social and cultural centre, by a project largely run by out of work school leavers.

Starter's Café is part of Shire Training Workshops, a project set up by a group of local individuals concerned for the future of school leavers, who are entering

a world which appears to have lost any clear understanding of the meaning and value of work. A local careers officer has complained that they are making work look too attractive ; STW consider that to be the kind of attitude that is giving work a bad name. The project is geared to instilling a sense of purpose in work, whatever the work might be, and to restoring to its tarnished image a sense of both self respect and social responsibility.

The initial group—they included a woodworker, a management consultant, a gardener, a child care officer and a teacher—pooled their resources, and found a building due for demolition in Stroud High Street to serve as their base. They obtained a grant from the Manpower Services Commission, and the local careers office began to send them trainees, who stay with them for up to one year.

Staff and trainees worked together to bring their old building alive ; now, the administration unit functions upstairs, a building project is in progress on the

Giving work a good name

At noon every seat is already taken : solicitors, housewives, teenagers, business- | a wor clear

QUESTION MARK HANGING OVER STARTERS

THE PROPOSED redevelopment of buildings in Stroud's High Street, which would mean demolition of the Starters Cafe building, has left a question mark on the future of the Shire Training Work-

Local and national press coverage and fundraising events from the early days of Shire Training Workshops

THE FRONT of No. 57, known until recently as Starters Cafe and having a long history of social concern.

Interesting features
of Number 57

future of Nos. 57 to 62 in Stroud High Street again recent report by Mr. Stanley Jones on No. 57 makes

New home for STW

troud's British School to be the new home Shire Training Work-ps.

spokesman for the .W. told the "News Journal" last week t contracts were with citors and it was ed that they would

Workshops developed a scheme to bring working skills — and more importantly, hope and self-respect — to unemployed school leavers.

It set up Starters Cafe in one of the High Street shops scheduled for demolition and against all

Co-op building at Cains-cross. But such was Shire Training Work-shops' impact on the town that Stroud District Council spent a great deal of time at its October meeting, discussing ways in which the

themselves" — and course, they were. Ev while the council we talking, Shire Traini Workshops were quie negotiating for the Br ish School.

Built in 1840, the Br ish School is a large.

The funding for the YOP scheme was managed by the Manpower Services Commission and the co-ordinator for Gloucestershire was very supportive and interested in this first project and very much on the side of Shire Training from the outset. Much needed funds were also raised from auctions, events and sales: local Quakers raised funds, and events included performances from internationally known poets Allen Ginsberg, Brian Patten and Michael Horovitz. Dr Fosters, Zippo the Clown and local band Blurt performed in the courtyard at the back. The project brought together arts and food and culture and building.

Within a few months the building team project managers couldn't eat there; at lunch time the queue would go way up the High Street.

Within the first year it was estimated that there were over twenty different local groups meeting there each week. Different philosophies were interacting, a fairly radical feminist and left-wing element, Christian socialism, Steiner anthroposophy and to some degree Quaker and ecological concerns. Patrick recalls, 'We ourselves were meeting weekly to manage the project, and then we'd meet again as a charity company meeting, and then we had a lot of ideas meetings. We'd be meeting sometimes three or four times a week.'

The consistent idea behind the project was that young people could do real work. The young people worked equally in the café, running the office services and on the building teams. Some of the young people had never made their own food, some had never been into the countryside. One young person had lived on the Bisley Road all her life, but never been to Bisley, let alone to carpeted shops in Cheltenham. Patrick still remembers driving a group up the Slad Valley when lambing was in full progress and the alarmed question: 'What are all those cats doing there?' By the end of nine months 30 young people signed up.

New staff were needed and Johann, a master craftsman from Holland, turned up one day covered in plaster and said, 'Boss, I want this job, I want to give something back, I'm 54 years old and I really want it.' The building projects included working with Andrew Wood developing the chapel in Uley which became

Prema; working at the Camphill in the Forest of Dean; landscaping at Newark Park; internal work at Edge church; working on private projects like restoring greenhouses, village hall repairs and building in France Lynch.

Starters was based in what is now Boots on the High Street. Four other buildings were empty and faced with demolition. The community agitation to save these semi-derelict buildings in the High Street was growing pace. Tom had copied the proposed plans for the five buildings and a letter was written that suggested that the planning officers were in cahoots with the demolition of the lower High Street. People started to occupy the roofs and Starters served 'Siege Pie'. Through this chaos they had a Manpower Services Commission inspection and the officer thought that all the action, the making and selling of food to campaigners and the young people's involvement in their town was a really good thing! A successful High Court case saved the buildings. Starters was given notice to quit.

Shire Training Workshops had their eyes on the British School, only recently saved from demolition by the cancelling of the Stroud Ring Road. They had to move to a couple of other places first but soon got that building; in 1980 it became a really imaginative building project for their teams. The courtyard was full of brambles – one of the young people just leapt in with a bill-hook and hacked his way out. There was a huge amount to do but over the next four years by 1984 they had become an established charity, had the governance, had a community adult scheme and young people's projects.

Funding programmes changed to the Youth Training Scheme and with it increased responsibilities and more restrictions to the work. Tom left then: 'We had set up something where the young people were equal workers with us. Margaret Thatcher then said there was no such thing as community. I just lost belief that the country would value its young people, would value its citizens not as economic units but as workers, as people who participated in building, doing community. I think the '80s, certainly the late '80s/90s, exactly showed the opposite.' George continues: 'It became very constricting. We were doing social and life skills but the government would no longer fund drama, they

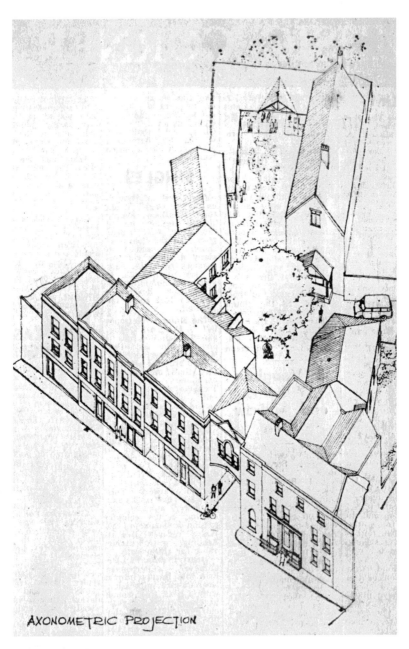

AXONOMETRIC PROJECTION

1980 vision for the yard behind what is now Boots, finally realised as Delmont's Lot in the late '90s

would no longer fund practical work projects in the community. It all became very structured and it was losing something. It's often the way with government schemes, they are very innovative to start with and then they get more and more politicised and they get more and more controlled, narrowed. And yet there were young people and there was a need and it was still a very good scheme. So I carried on but at a certain point I thought actually now is the time for me to leave and for other people to take it on, and so I left in 1985.'

In 1988 the YTS scheme that had been run by STW was finally closed down. Many individuals who had worked so hard within the scheme were forced to leave. Karen Baker, who had been much involved in the work of STW, stayed on helping avert an even deeper crisis of the charity. Lucas Shoemaker stepped in and for a while they worked together as co-administrator/managers. However it was under difficult circumstances, resources were tight and Karen eventually withdrew and Lucas continued on a part-time basis, trying to hold things together and find a way forward.

Lucas too was part of the Emerson College group and had known Tom there in the mid-'70s; they met again at Starters Café. Lucas had become one of the building project managers in 1982 and a trustee in '83. By 1987 the whole project was on the verge of collapse when the Manpower Services Commission changed its method of working and all contracts were to go to large colleges rather than to individual charities like Shire Training Workshops.

There were around four years of really searching for projects. There was just no funding for working with young people. Stroud College ran the café for a while, a women's returner group was run and the office team continued. There were debates about removing the anthroposophical side of the constitution but the Charities Commission said that money would have to be returned if they changed that fundamental aspect of the project. Rooms in the building were hired out. A mortgage had been raised to pay the redundancy payments in '87 and the finances were really perilous. The early '90s recession was coming. There were no more government schemes, there was no more money, so there were no young people being trained through these years. The British

School was used for a lot of events, concerts, artists' workshops and so on, and so it felt like a thriving venue, central to Stroud's cultural activities. Lucas was only being paid one or two days a week and really wanted some kind of change to happen. Others too were working hard for the charity voluntarily or for minimal pay.

One day, in the autumn of 1992, he and Roger Budgeon, then setting up his eco shop at his garage in Bisley, took a walk around Stroud to look at possibilities and talk about ideas. Lucas takes up the story: 'Roger said, "If you had this pub, The Painswick Inn, as well as the British School, then you would have a whole corner of buildings; you could have people living upstairs and working downstairs. You would have some critical mass." I said, "Well, fat chance, we've got a building with a high mortgage, no money." Lo and behold, three months later, the pub comes up for sale. The landlord has run off, the building is boarded up and up for sale – £75,000. So I phone Roger up and tell him that the Whitbread-run pub is up for sale! Any ideas? And he said, "I serviced a car belonging to the Whitbread executive in Cheltenham." He talks to them. And he gets an option to buy, six months to get the money together. We had to turn up with £37,000 for the first stage.

'So then there is a meeting with the Trustees, the idea of turning it into a homeless hostel and then workshops maybe downstairs. Others also saw great potential in acquiring the Painswick Inn but felt if charitable funding was to be attracted, a much stronger vision was needed of how the building could be used for and by the homeless and unemployed young people of Stroud. Lucas stepped back and a small group – Patrick Mansfield, Mary Lettington and Roger Budgeon – took the project forward for around two months. On 20 January 1993 they got an article on the front page of the Stroud News & Journal outlining a vision and appealing for support. Patrick well remembers the call from Roger ten days later saying that the article had just helped attract £30,000 towards the project.

Lucas realised that the finances would work, 'I phoned Roger up, and I said this is bonkers, isn't it? Because it's 10 bedrooms. I could rent each bedroom

Top: Restoring the Badbrook culvert as part of the renovation of the British School, early '80s
Bottom: Slad Road frontage to the British School

out for £40 a week. That's £400 a week, isn't it? That's £20,000 a year. It's a doddle, isn't it? Surely, we can get something together? Roger and I meet and we say we have got to raise the rest of the money in two weeks. So we do!'

Roger wrote a solid, long-term business plan: building the business on IT courses, building a property base, being part of the statutory delivery service, working with housing associations, working with the District Council. This business plan and raising the money from local well-wishers 'really got us motoring'.

It was all happening at the right moment. There were funds for young people's housing and in the mid-'90s the new Lottery funding also came on stream. Young people filled the residential vacancies from the moment they were ready. The Lottery funding enabled there to be courses and learning support linked to the residential work. More office space was needed and 48 High Street came up for sale in 2002 and was set up as offices for GloFysh (Gloucestershire Young People's Housing), with the Social Enterprise centre behind it and more flats for young people upstairs, who were moving on from Ruskin Mill. And then the warehouse behind Boots – the venue for those early Starters gigs – came up and more housing was made available. The little Smartworks building was taken on and done up across the road from the British School. Millions of pounds were raised over 10 years and four significant buildings in Stroud had been restored to full use.

The funding that supported the young people's learning was increasingly all focused on qualifications (and still is). Andrew Thirkettle joined the organisation and had real skills in blending training, learning and qualifications. He also worked with Lucas on funding applications and the whole project changed from near collapse to a hive of industry, work and support for young people.

The government funding schemes lurched from one focus to another. Also the young people coming had more and more difficulties and more support needs as other projects and courses skimmed off the more able of them. This decade from the mid-'90s was one of constant change, new initiatives, always wanting 'innovation', endless funding streams, moving the goalposts and saying that 16 to 25 is OK, then 16 to 19 only. When asked what was the most difficult thing about running an organisation for so long, Lucas said: 'To meet the ever-changing goalposts of government. To come up with new ways of formatting the service so it would fit the criteria the government had set. To meet the ever more head space-orientated qualifications of education the government sees as needed whereas we see that the young people and certainly the young men are screaming out for practical work. And all these people need art and creativity to express themselves and can then make a wonderful contribution to the lives of people; that's not appreciated by government. It's all about the qualifications. And that's the hard part.'

Lucas was exhausted after three decades with Shire Training Workshops and left in 2011. 'Shire is very much about being in town, in the community. I was really delighted that young people can be living so centrally in a town. That was a real achievement.'

For a new Chief Executive, in fact only the second one that Shire Training Workshops has had, coming into a well-established organisation is a challenge. But that challenge is interesting for any organisation – what to change, what to keep and a fresh pair of eyes on how the organisation is seen from other agencies and funders. Dr Claire Mould's first job as Chief Executive was to do an in-depth appraisal with the young people, with the staff, with the trustees and especially with people on the outside looking in. She found that some people knew of Shire Training Workshops very well – but it was a small coterie of people despite the long years of its presence. The many name changes over the decades (although needed at the time) did not help – some people knew it as the British School, others as Five Valleys Foyer, others as The Painswick Inn Project. It was time for a new name and with the help of a marketing expert the new name of OPENhouse was chosen to reflect the service that is offered to young people: residential help and life skills support as well as an organisation that is open to ideas and to collaboration.

Claire was really pleased that the original objectives, set in 1978, were still

Top: Delmont's Lot, upgraded in 2012
Bottom: Delmont's Lot, new vegetable gardens

core. That very impetus of making a project with young people who feel disenfranchised, which had so exercised the founders, was as relevant in 2011 as then.

Claire then ensured that she and the work of OPENhouse became well known. She knows that contacts and profile-raising across the county and through the complex web of statutory and voluntary sector organisations that support young people in Gloucestershire is essential for the long-term success of the project. She sits on a number of boards with the County Council commissioning teams. She is the Voluntary Community Sector (VCS) ambassador and on the Board of the Local Enterprise Partnership, the VCS representative on the Vale and Valleys Partnership, and Chair of the Gloucestershire VCS Alliance.

She says: 'The staff were doing some amazing work and had exceptional skills with young people with autism and Asperger's, but this was not really known. Now that we are boxing above our weight the staff recognise their value as well and are keen to raise their own expertise and consolidate the quality of the service.

'We are a specialist service for people with Asperger's and autism, at a time where funding for support with autism is dropping off in the county. We felt so strongly about something we'd been doing for a number of years that we set up an Asperger's group here run by the service users themselves and we trained peer mentors within that. Holding onto the quality of that work is now bringing in the funding and a good reputation and now we have been asked to take the lead in a large consortium on autism. This has been a really hard time for funding – all the payments are now on results and commissioners want to bring in big organisations. The move is very much away from small, local charities.'

Claire recognised that dropping out of education really affects young people. Over the past two years the organisation has built up the education side – not just what is offered at OPENhouse, although that is essential and very creative, but also working across all the agencies – schools, exclusions, extended learning.

Young people now in threat of exclusion can come one day a week or for a full week's programme to OPENhouse and still maintain a link with their own school. Funding supports both the school and OPENhouse and their education service now caters for pupils from 14 upwards. This is a really important service and new to the District.

The main age group with regard to education at OPENhouse is 16–19, although that can be extended if someone has very particular support needs, but it is important not to put everyone together until they feel really confident. A new aspect of the project is everyone having lunch together – Open Lunches! That's a free lunch for everybody, Sunshine bakery giving free rolls and OPENhouse providing fruit and ham and salad and juice and such so that everybody can sit together informally. The resonances with the early days are very strong here – good food, nourishing food, and sharing and eating together are needed as much now as in the late '70s. Some of the young people have not had breakfast and are living on Haribos, energy drinks and nicotine. This is an important part of the day for them and a band called Sick Wave, made up of OPENhouse music students, has developed from meeting at these lunches.

At Christmas everyone wanted a traditional cooked lunch so they all joined in, sorted out the decorations, helped with the cooking, arranged music and had a huge, social, community meal together. Remember, these are young people often with fractured backgrounds, they do not eat well, they do not socialise easily.

Off the back of that event, lunches are now being cooked regularly at the Delmont's Lot lovely new kitchen. This has become a whole new focus for OPENhouse – growing food, eating food, learning cooking skills. 'We are starting a community café there as a social enterprise with donations for the food,' says Claire. This café recognises that loneliness and marginalisation are big things for many people and links are being made across different organisations so that their contacts can know about the café. It's a place where people can sit for a long while. They can be involved in the garden if they wish. They do not need to spend a lot of money.

There are 20 young people involved in the education side, with very high levels of staff support. 10 young people live in the old Painswick Inn – they are the 16-year-olds who have nowhere else to go. After 18 months or so, when they are confident, they can move into smaller flats further up the High Street. Other people are living independently but linked to OPENhouse. There are also young people with mental health issues, needing support: some living together, some independently, and OPENhouse is changing Delmont's Lot into a supportive, residential house for those young people – a safe community but in town, not isolated and separate. All the young people bring a different story – some are very resilient, need OPENhouse but are keen to go to College and are thinking positively about their futures. Others need a lot of support over the years. 'What we do is completely person-centred, completely bespoke to the individual,' says Claire. 'There aren't two people that have the same programme, whether that be in the house, whether that be through our mental health support, or whether that be through learning – no two people are the same.'

Finances continue to be tough. Some people view OPENhouse as integral to the Steiner community and supported by that community. Although some of the founding principles are Steiner, OPENhouse raises all its own funding. Others think that owning four buildings must mean there are funds. However, listed buildings can be expensive to upkeep and rents are kept low for community and small business use. Balancing the books is always tricky and these are difficult times for an organisation that is developing new services and new ideas and is looking to a long-term sustainable future.

The Stroud community generally is supportive of the work, with good links made to Fairshares, Star Anise, the Stroud Half Marathon, Stroud Valleys Project. However, what seems to be the most attractive part of OPENhouse to local people are the education and creative programmes. Claire says, 'I don't think people are aware that we really struggle with funding to make sure that young people get a cooked meal every day – and this is on their doorstep. I am not sure people know how many homeless young people there are in Stroud and just how bad their mental health issues can be. We need to be addressing

OPENhouse creative workshop

these issues and involving others and that is what our community kitchen aims to do.'

When looking to that future Claire says, 'There are an awful lot of people who can't wait until they are 16 to find a safe place to live, so where are they going to go? We've got a lot of work to do with regard to the homeless agenda. We need to look at the ways in which we can be supporting and campaigning for our homeless young people and looking to support those young people. They may never be able to afford to live on their own, so supporting them to be able to live in shared accommodation is the most effective way.'

Interviewees: *Tom Bermingham, Patrick Mansfield, Dr Claire Mould, George Perry, Lucas Shoemaker*

Below: The High Street is carried through Stroud in a coffin
Bottom: The Medieval Hall at the top of the High Street, early '80s

3 The 1980s

Stroud Preservation Trust 1982

'When I look back, this [the Toll House, Cainscross] wasn't the project that I would say was the one I was most proud of but despite it only being a tiny little project it made a huge difference to the landscape and local people were very, very pleased. We had rescued a building from all its scaffolding and we got lots of positive comments.'

Anne Mackintosh, Trustee and founding member

STROUD PRESERVATION TRUST HAS been part of a very tangible change in Stroud, both physical and cultural, over the past 35 years. The campaigns around the bypass and the High Street were the foundation stones for Stroud Preservation Trust, as they were for Shire Training Workshops, and are dealt with in some detail in this chapter. These campaigns and the subsequent work of Stroud Preservation Trust and other organisations helped to change how Stroud looks and how it functions as a town.

Four decades ago, the High Street was choked with traffic negotiating the narrow, steep street and blighted by empty and derelict buildings, some held up by scaffolding and patched with corrugated iron. Two successful campaigns, both focused on saving listed buildings, helped to lay the foundations for this transformation. Firstly, although many agreed that pedestrianisation and a new road system were needed, the County Council's proposals for a ring road were controversial and there was a successful and hard fought campaign for a different solution. The intended first ring road scheme and subsequent revised proposals had a major impact upon Stroud for over twenty years from the 1960s to the 1980s. Secondly, the dramatic High Street siege campaign, which saved a swathe of listed buildings, lead to a landmark legal judgement and the foundation of the Stroud Preservation Trust.

There had been proposals by Gloucestershire County Council for a ring road for Stroud since 1959, and by 1965 a plan had been developed. The proposed route would have required the demolition of listed buildings and divided the main commercial area of town from residential areas. The proposal was to widen Merrywalks and demolish the listed 18th-century police station at Beeches Green and the British School. As the road turned towards Slad, it was to go up 20 feet on stilts, 'the Slad flyover', and skim past another listed building, the old museum on Lansdown, now the Centre for Arts and Science. It would then head up the hill, going close to St Laurence's Church, under the new police station, to cut across more old buildings at the top of the High Street and then down to join the London Road. By the 1970s, according to an article in *The Architect's Journal* (August 1975), there were also related proposals to demolish 19th-century buildings on Lansdown to make way for a shop and office development to link up with the newly built Merrywalks shopping centre.

For 15 years these gaps and increasingly derelict empty buildings became a classic case of planning blight, contributing to Stroud's commercial decline. By the time 'incomers' started to fight against the ring road, buildings had already been demolished along Slad Road (where Locking Hill Surgery is now), plus four houses on Lansdown (just recently rebuilt), a little house near the Church, and High Street buildings above what is now the last shop on the left at the top of the High Street.

This was a hard-fought campaign against the new road with primary leaders Clare Toy and Mary Fermor learning the ropes at every step. The campaign culminated in a Public Inquiry in 1976, which centred on whether consents to demolish listed buildings to make way for the road should be granted. The Inspector found there was no case to demolish these buildings as the proposed ring road would be an 'environmental disaster'. An alternative proposal was accepted: an east–west bypass linking the A46 Bath Road and the A419 London Road, passing along part of the route of the canal, finally built in 1987 and known as Dr Newton's Way. The campaign was run by local people, volunteering their time; mostly these people were new to Stroud. They could see some potential in this ravaged and semi-derelict little town and they ran imaginative actions like lining up people holding poles to show the extraordinary heights that the Slad flyover would have taken. This simple action gave people a real idea of what the intended road would look like – often very hard to read from a map or plan.

Mike Goodenough, Steve Tomlin and Julian Usborne led the battle to save some decaying listed buildings at 57–62 High Street (now the four shops down from Boots the Chemist). The 17th- and 18th-century buildings had been bought up over several years by Milwards, a shoe retailer, in order to convert the block into modern shop units. An application for planning consent for the redevelopment of the buildings was turned down in 1977. The plan was pretty radical. All the buildings would be pulled down, new shops built and a large concrete ramp from the High Street would run behind the shops for lorry deliveries at first floor level. At a public meeting where the developers wanted to put forward their proposals the Subscription Rooms were completely packed. 'The scheme was so awful that a really large movement started against it,' says Anne Mackintosh, who joined the campaign as Treasurer.

In March 1980, Stroud District Council took an action under the 1936 Public Health Act under which 60 and 61 High Street were declared dangerous and Milwards, given the option to repair or demolish the property, decided to demolish. The Civic Society had already been working to save the buildings and now the Stroud High Street Action Group was formed using Starters Café (in what is now Boots) as one of their regular meeting venues. The buildings could have been lost because of a legal loophole: public health legislation appeared to allow demolition. It seemed that owners could leave a property to become dangerous and then legally demolish it. There was no application for listed building consent to demolish until days before the demolition was due to begin.

The protesters saved the buildings through a combination of direct and High Court actions, showing great verve and resourcefulness. Protests and processions in the High Street culminated in two rooftop occupations of 60 and 61 High Street to prevent demolition as contractors made ready to start work. The second occupation came after a High Court direction given on 3 June 1980, that Stroud District Council should reconsider all the statutory powers open to it to make owners maintain listed buildings as the protection of   listed buildings took precedence over provisions for the demolition under the Public Health Act. The case (R v. Stroud District Council ex parte Goodenough, Usborne and Tomlin) was subsequently quoted in a Department of Environment Circular and legal textbooks and was considered a great step forward in the conservation world. 'It was amazing to us that the two judges at the High Court really wanted to understand our position. They listened and then they made the judgement in our favour,' says Mike Goodenough.

However, the District Council did not take any action. On 10 June demolition workers began stripping the roofs but found themselves at the centre of another wave of protest as the High Street filled with demonstrators, some of whom climbed scaffolding at the rear of the buildings to begin a second roof top occupation. The affair attracted plenty of local and some national press interest.

NEWS & JOURNAL, TH

Stroud High Street Inquiry:
CONSERVATIONISTS PUT THEIR CASE

STROUD'S HISTORICAL High Street buildings are an "integral part of the town's heritage" and should be saved at any cost, Cheltenham conservationist, Dr. Paul Saunders, said last week.

Stroud District Council, under pressure, accepted legal advice that the only demolition of a listed building that should be allowed under public health legislation is the minimum needed to make the building safe. Milwards then withdrew their application to demolish and eventually the buildings were restored and made suitable for modern use.

Stroud Preservation Trust was founded against this background of plans, protest and people willing to take action: 'To preserve for the benefit of the townspeople of Stroud...and of the nation at large...buildings of particular beauty or historical, architectural or constructional interest.'

At the Public Inquiry into the ring road, the Inspector had recommended that the listed buildings at the (now) top of the High Street should not be demolished as they were 'of particular interest because they appear to contain the oldest structural features from the time when Stroud was centred on The Cross'.

In 1980, the Stroud Preservation Trust's founders commissioned a survey by an architectural historian, Stanley Jones, which revealed that, behind its Georgian facade, 33 High Street was indeed an extremely rare survival, an urban medieval hall. The roof timbers were typically medieval and heavily coated in soot, probably from smoke from a central hearth when the building was open to the roof. In the same year, the County Council produced draft proposals to build a relief road from The Cross to London Road (Cornhill, eventually built in the mid-1980s). These proposals again threatened the Medieval Hall but it was recognised as important and was donated by the County Council to Stroud Preservation Trust for £1. The buildings above the Medieval Hall, numbers 35–37 High Street, were lost to make way for the link road, which caused some controversy, but the relief road allowed the High Street to be pedestrianised at last.

The Medieval Hall became the first project for Stroud Preservation Trust, which was formally constituted as a charity in 1982. Founder member Anne Mackintosh, who had been the treasurer for the Stroud High Street Action Group, remembers, 'I had three young children, my youngest was at nursery and the other two at school. It was a perfect time for me to get involved in this town which I liked. It was very exciting. I didn't sit on the High Street shop roofs but made sure everyone had plenty of refreshments and sleeping bags!'

Stroud Preservation Trust wanted to prove that it was possible to turn a derelict and ancient building into an asset to the town. They did not have an easy task ahead of them. Anne Macktintosh explains: 'It was frightening, it was absolutely frightening and I had utterly no idea of what I would be doing. Luckily, through Mike Goodenough we had met Richard Feilden. He was young and had a small architect's practice, Feilden Clegg Design Partnership, and he was very, very keen on the Medieval Hall. Richard did some research and found out a lot about Building Preservation Trusts, and we also found out about the Manpower Service Commission who were giving grants if you employed people. We got them to agree to have twelve people employed, one of whom was a bookkeeper.'

Left: The Medieval Hall in disrepair
Right: The Manpower Services team working on the Medieval Hall

It was not a straightforward construction project. The demolition of the adjacent buildings caused major technical and architectural problems as a new facade had to be constructed down one side. It was difficult to make plans of the building as it stood, due to its dilapidation and a complex structure that had been altered and adapted over the centuries. Also, some features were revealed only as gutting and restoration took place. It was therefore also hard to draw up a detailed schedule of work. The team of labourers who worked on the building were long-term unemployed and it was not easy to manage a disparate and largely unskilled team of workers on a difficult and sometimes dangerous building site. Julian Usborne did all the building project management and Anne Mackintosh supported the workers.

Gradually the workers did become a team and the job was done over 18 months, from March 1981 to September 1982. 'When it was finished it was gorgeous, we couldn't believe how wonderful it looked,' says Anne. On completion, 32–34 High Street was transformed into a handsome and distinctive building with three shops, two office units and a pleasant courtyard area.

Stroud Preservation Trust had shown what could be done and perhaps begun to change some minds about the worth of restoring old buildings. A Department of Environment inspector for historic buildings described the project as 'the most encouraging thing to come out of Stroud in thirty years'.

Anne Mackintosh continues: 'I never thought we would do another building but within months Julian was negotiating for 55 High Street, now Moonflower, which had to be sold in a hurry.' This handsome and prominent building was in a poor state of repair and marred by an unsympathetic modern shop front. The derelict top floors had been unused and inaccessible for years. The property was in the right location and condition for the Trust to show the benefits of a sensitive and practical approach to building conservation. The Trust bought the property and developed over two years an imaginative and sympathetic scheme, which provided a large shop facing the High Street, four flats above the shop and opened up the old alleyway to the yard behind. This alleyway provides access to two further shops, Mills Café, the Health Centre and the courtyard with outside seating. The project is a visual and commercial success, which cleverly maximised the potential of the site. Many of the new, local and independent businesses who first moved in are still there and thriving. Soon after 55 High Street was completed, the High Street was finally pedestrianised. A contemporary article in a local magazine commented that: 'The optimism generated by the success of Withey's Yard seems to be infectious… The High Street has lost its air of shabbiness, which is strange because it is hard to see what exactly has changed.'

These two projects really boosted the confidence of Stroud Preservation Trust. They knew that the historic value of a building was essential knowledge when compiling early reports and feasibility studies; they worked with experts to help develop the best results for buildings; they understood how important it was to run a well-managed charity and abide by charity law. These are steps learned by all organisations through experience and they support success.

Stroud Preservation Trust went on to restore the Cainscross Toll House and 1 Bridge Street, purchased in August 1987 from the Gloucester and Severnside Co-operative Society after lengthy negotiations. 'When I look back, this wasn't the project that I would say was the one I was most proud of but despite it only being a tiny little project it made a huge difference to the landscape and local people were very, very pleased. We had rescued a building from all its scaffolding and we got lots of positive comments,' says Anne.

Stroud Preservation Trust was on a roll. Their finances were building up and there was a lot of property to look at and discover in the valleys. Anne Mackintosh remembers the next project: 'We bought Arundel because it was falling down and nobody else could have saved it.' Arundel Mill House and Cottages were in a ruinous state when Stroud Preservation Trust bought them in February 1990. The buildings were obscured by invasive undergrowth and riddled with wet rot and furniture beetle. Cracks in the walls visibly widened during the months when the Trust was negotiating to buy. Once the sale of the property was completed, emergency work began the same day to prop up the Mill House. This was a large, complex and expensive project, which took three years

The Arundel Mill cottages before and after renovation

to complete. Some land on the site was sold to help finance the restoration.

The one-acre property included the Mill House, an adjoining workshop and two semi-detached cottages. The Trust's scheme provided seven homes on the site with private and communal gardens. A joint project with Stroud Valleys Project rebuilt the broken weir and restored the large mill pond. Stroud Valleys Project continue to manage the pond. From a near ruin to secluded housing in a serene setting, this ambitious project was a real success.

The Trust had also taken on the Goods Shed in Station Yard. This was proving to be a difficult project to move on and after its first essential restoration (new roof, restored stone and essential repairs and windows) various projects and ideas were developed to a high standard but none came to fruition. Most of the '90s was spent revisiting the Trust's purpose. Arundel Mill had cost a great deal and the early '90s economic recession meant that the project only just covered costs and no profits were made. The Goods Shed project ideas also suffered from the recession – a great deal of funding was needed to bring the shed into active use and it was owned by Network Rail, not the Trust, so there would be little or no financial benefit from an end user.

The '90s went on with the Goods Shed as a primary focus and with many small projects of feasibility studies and support work for other buildings in the valleys. Anne Mackintosh was also a trustee for Stroud Valleys Project and gave enormous time to that project as well as to the Community Planning Project. Gradually the buildings in the valleys were being taken on and improved and prices were rising and rising, putting many properties out of reach of the Trust's now limited funds. Stroud Preservation Trust was often asked to be involved in building projects – advice on the Old Town Hall saw its renovation when the District Council moved out; a private buyer took on all the flats above Kendrick Street and brought in many more people to live in the town; the Co-op changed plans for what is now the Factory Shop on Westward Road because of SPT advice, and Anne Mackintosh supported St Albans church through the consistory court. SPT's chair for 25 years, Nigel Paterson, also worked with a small group of people on the Gloucestershire Buildings

Recording Group, which collected masses of information about the vernacular buildings of the county. This expertise along with the learning curves from each project put Stroud Preservation Trust in the centre of restoration and planning for the area.

During 2000 –1 grant funds were raised to celebrate and renovate the Anti-Slavery Arch,which stands on the corner of the Paganhill Estate in Stroud and gives Archway School its name. This is the only memorial of its type left in Britain to the abolition of slavery in the British Colonies. It was built in 1834 as the grand entrance to a Georgian mansion, Farmhill Park, by its new owner Henry Wyatt. The house, carriage drive and gates are gone, leaving the classical arch with its diminutive lodge house. Due to its particular historic interest, in 2007 the monument was upgraded from a Grade II listing to Grade II*.

A local group, 'The Anti-Slavery Arch Group', led by Anne Mackintosh of Stroud Preservation Trust, raised funds of £25,000 for a community project. This included major stone repairs to the arch and works to the footpath, a bronze plaque, a leaflet and a community play. Archway School used the restoration of the Arch to highlight the plight of modern day slavery.

By 2013 the Trust had been custodian of the Goods Shed for over a quarter of a century. The signing of the sublease with Stroud Valleys Artspace in May 2011 was the culmination of years of persistent hard work by members of the Trust, raising funds, maintaining and improving the building, and negotiating with possible users.

The Goods Shed was built in 1845 to a standard design by Isambard Kingdom Brunel, and is now the only survivor of this type. Until 1966, the Goods Shed was used as covered accommodation for unloading and transferring goods to road vehicles – at first horse-drawn carts and later lorries. Out of use, the building was open and vulnerable and fell into disrepair. In 1984 British Rail removed the slate roof, which had become dangerous to the public. The building was listed Grade II in 1985 at the request of Stroud Preservation Trust and upgraded to Grade II* in 1989.

Left: Brunel Goods Shed repairs, 1988
Middle: Goods Shed re-roofed, internal view
Bottom: Sunday Telegraph reporting the
Goods Shed shortlisted for the Angel Awards

Category two | **Best rescue of an industrial building**

Brunel Goods Shed, Gloucestershire

○ Only Isambard Kingdom Brunel could have chosen to build a railway shed in the Tudor Gothic revival style, complete with miniature flying buttresses.

steel shutters had to be installed to protect it against vandals.

How does this story end? With a proposal by a local arts group to use the shed as a base for a Carnival Collective. But first the electrics and plumbing have

producti
being the
million to
Key to its
reliabilit
and that t
continued,

*Top: Stroud Valleys Artspace event
at the Goods Shed, 2011
Middle: Gloucestershire's
sailing Olympics launch, 2012
Bottom: Stroud Life reporting SVA's signing
of a five-year lease for the Goods Shed*

Once a busy interchange, essential to the local economy, by the 1980s the Goods Shed was a neglected, redundant building. However, this elegant, industrial structure designed by one of England's greatest engineers had been considered a possible project soon after Stroud Preservation Trust was formed. In 1986, after two years of complex negotiations, the Trust agreed a 40-year lease with British Rail. Fundraising began with the appeal patron being Reverend W. Awdry, author of the *Thomas the Tank Engine* books, who had retired to Rodborough. Major repairs and improvements, including a new slate roof, stonework repairs and installation of some services, were carried out in 1988 at a cost of £130,000. The Goods Shed had been rescued from dereliction but needed a user to secure its future.

There was no shortage of ideas or interest in the Goods Shed. There had been proposals that the building become a theatre, a restaurant, an antiques and arts centre, offices, a museum, a Real Tennis court, bus and coach storage and indoor cricket school, to name a few. Proposals didn't go ahead because the costs of alteration were too high, the building was not suitable or because the required changes were not acceptable to English Heritage. Stroud Preservation Trust entered into discussions on all these suggestions and commissioned feasibility studies of its own. By the start of the new millennium, all proposals were hampered by a possible new transport interchange in the station area, which would have entailed major redevelopment.

Throughout this time the building, which was on English Heritage's Buildings at Risk register for many years, was open and subject to vandalism such as graffiti, broken windows, fires and stone quarrying. Meanwhile, work continued to find a user and by 2010, Stroud Preservation Trust's trustees decided to at least secure the building in order to both protect it and make it more attractive to possible users. The building was closed with roller shutters, a raised floor was created over the track and an external platform removed and replaced with a smaller balcony. The £129,000 project was funded with major grants from the Railway Heritage Trust, Stroud District Council, Stroud Town Council and the Gloucestershire Environment Trust and other donors. At last it was off the Buildings at Risk list, was enclosed and had a wonderful floor covering nearly 4,000 sq feet. There was three-phase electricity and running water for the first time in its history.

In May 2011, Stroud Preservation Trust were delighted to sign an initial five-year sub lease to Stroud Valleys Artspace, who are using the Goods Shed for all kinds of artistic and educational projects. Carnival preparations, art installations, performances and exhibitions, film and music shows have all been held at the Goods Shed. Some of the offices are now used by artists.

Over the years six buildings have been rescued from dereliction by Stroud Preservation Trust and currently provide six flats, ten houses, six shops, two offices, one café, one natural health centre and one arts venue. These historic buildings, once seen as dilapidated eyesores, have become assets to Stroud. As well as looking good, they play their part in Stroud's economic, social and cultural life.

Harder to quantify, but undoubtedly true, is the catalyst effect whereby the example set by the Trust's work has led to improvements to other buildings. The early projects in the High Street showed that some people valued Stroud's past and had faith in its future. They helped to win the support of the public and Stroud District Council for a conservation-led approach to regeneration. The restored buildings encouraged others to make physical improvements. After 32–34 High Street was finished, many shopkeepers painted their shops for the first time in years. At Cainscross, after the Toll House had been restored, the old empty Co-op building was sold and converted into shops, a workshop and flats. The Withey's Yard development showed what could be done with the area behind a shop and provided space for the first outside café seating in Stroud. That imaginative approach to the restoration and use of historic buildings has brought innovations to Stroud. Private developers and other projects have tackled buildings with real enthusiasm and skill, and the town has changed beyond all measure from the High Street of 40 years ago with its snarled traffic, empty building lots, scaffolding and dereliction.

Interviewees: *Anne Mackintosh, Mike Goodenough*

Restored buildings, clockwise from top left: the Medieval Hall, 55 High Street, Arundel Mill House, the Goods Shed, the Anti-Slavery Arch, the Cainscross Toll House

The 1980s

4 | Stroud Valleys Project 1987

'The catalyst for SVP came from a report commissioned by Stroud District Council in 1985 from an organisation called Urbed to look at the use of all the old mills along the valleys. That's how we ended up with our name 'Stroud Valleys Project', because originally the mills were, obviously, strung out along the valleys. The report identified the mills as of enormous value, because they were key, they thought, to the rejuvenation of the Stroud area. And also they didn't want to lose the historical connections. After that report the mills were referred to in the press as 'The String of Pearls', a catch phrase that has stuck. So that's the catalyst for the organisation starting off.'

Stella Parkes, SVP Trustee and former Chair

2013 IS STROUD VALLEYS PROJECT'S 25th birthday. Since 1988, the organisation has protected and enhanced the local built and natural environment by working with local communities around Stroud to embrace sustainable development and biodiversity. The influence of Stroud and its history of community action is of course strong, and SVP has acted as a catalyst for many different protests and actions across the District.

'I think the reason we're still here after 25 years is that we've changed and evolved with the times,' says Clare Mahdiyone, SVP's current chief executive. When the Stroud Valleys Project was set up, it was constituted so that all its 12 trustees were representatives of other organisations around the area – the idea being that they could all work together jointly on projects for the community. However, this was changed later on and, although there is still a representative from Stroud District Council (SDC), other organisations are no longer represented. Currently there are seven trustees, with Gerry Robbins as their chair. Clare, who has worked at SVP since 2006, summarises the organisation's ethos this way: 'One of the things we try to do is take a national idea and make it work at a local level, so that you get the involvement of individuals and communities, and everybody works together. I think that's what is strong about the work we do. It's about bringing people together and about them being able to learn things – based on the environment as the main part of the work.'

The organisation received money at first from both the County and District Councils, and has always been majority grant-funded. There is, however, a constant worry about money. 'That's the constant fight – to keep going,' says Stella Parkes, a SVP trustee and former chair. There are eight paid employees at the time of writing; the number of staff depends on the projects they're doing and the funding available.

Stella has been involved with Stroud Valleys Project almost since the very beginning. She started off working there when Chris Smith, the first Project Officer, was in charge and did some PR work for them when they put the new lock gates in at Wallbridge and when they restored the Georgian bridge at Lodgemore Mills. Then she went on to do a survey called Living Above the Shop: the District Council had given SVP some grant money to look at all the spaces above the shops in Stroud and see if they could be turned into living accommodation.

Looking back, Stella recalls the early days: 'The catalyst for SVP came from a report commissioned by Stroud District Council in 1985 from an organisation called Urbed [Urbanism Environment Design] to look at the use of all the old mills along the valleys. That's how we ended up with our name "Stroud Valleys Project", because originally the mills were, obviously, strung out along the valleys. The report identified the mills as of enormous value, because they were key, they thought, to the rejuvenation of the Stroud area. And also they didn't want to lose the historical connections. After that report the mills were referred to in the press as 'The String of Pearls', a catch phrase that has stuck. So that's the catalyst for the organisation starting off.' The report had been written by Nick Falk of Urbed who lived in Stroud and attached to it were detailed drawings and descriptions of many of the 90 mills in the valleys, researched and produced by four of the people who had

The harvest and tools donation at Cam Everlands

built the cycle track from Stroud to Nailsworth. That MSC scheme employed two people as industrial archaeologists and two as environmentalists and their expertise fed into the Urbed report. A good example as to how projects build and share knowledge.

At that juncture the core of SVP was a group of driven individuals including Anne Mackintosh, Mike Goodenough and Peter Bateman who met weekly as a management committee. Meeting four or five times a year the Board represented a large number of local organisations, including the Chamber of Trade, Gloucestershire Trust for Nature Conservation, Stroud Preservation Trust, Stroud and District Civic Society, Stroud Action Group, Gloucestershire Society for Industrial Archaeology, Gloucestershire Wildlife Trust and Stroudwater, Thames and Severn Canal Trust.

'Board meetings were complex and very unwieldy, with a mixture of different kinds of individuals, pedalling in slightly different directions,' says Chris Smith, who joined SVP as their first Project Officer in 1989.

The aim at the beginning had been a focus on the industrial heritage of the area. Urbed's report identified certain mills as being of interest or at risk, the principal ones being Stanley, Ebley, Dunkirk, Ruskin, Kimmins, Belvedere and Bourne mills. The thrust of the report was based on the valleys' industrial heritage.

Mike Goodenough takes up the story: 'Most of the groups on the Board wanted to broaden the remit to include the built and natural heritage of the Stroud Valleys as a whole. You have to understand that many of us had been at odds with the council for years over its development and environmental policies and saw this as an opportunity for change. We also didn't have a Town Council at the time – it wasn't until 1990 that the Stroud Town Council was formed, so we'd been without any directly elected representatives since 1974.'

Mike recalls that the District Council didn't have much in-house expertise on listed buildings or conservation issues: 'What we wanted was something that was going to be more of a community development trust that would bring those resources together with people who had demonstrated their commitment at working to further the conservation of both the built and natural environment.'

A working group was set up which spent quite a lot of time arguing over the composition and remit of this proposed organisation. SDC organised a number of trips, to towns like Wirksworth, Calne and Hebden Bridge, all with similar problems to the ones the group had identified – most of which were to do with the causes and results of urban decay. SDC were keen to get on with setting a project up. 'I suppose from their point of view,' says Mike, 'we kept frustrating their efforts with our attempts to broaden the aims and objectives, and to establish better community representation.'

SDC wanted it to be a council-controlled body but were in a quandary because any development trust that was set up would need to be seen as independent, in order to attract outside funding. Gordon Michell of the Civic Trust, who had set up the ground-breaking Wirksworth Project and then had been instrumental in the Calne Project, came to Stroud to speak at a public meeting. 'He essentially said that SDC were mistaken if they thought they could do it their way,' says Mike, 'and that they would need to have the community actively involved in running it: you just had to trust people to do it. After that SDC really had no choice but to support a properly independent body.'

With some of the working group members, Mike wrote a policy document, which was an attempt to identify all the things they thought at the time were important and to suggest projects that might address some of those issues. 'It's interesting that people now seem to think that it was set up to protect buildings – that it was building-orientated,' he says, 'but reading the report again it's clear that it was always much broader than that. The report states that the first aim was "to establish a greater sense of awareness and pride in the uniqueness of the area". It seemed to most of us that the uniqueness of the area was its inextricable combination of buildings and nature and how you treated that would be hugely important to the future of the Stroud Valleys. Possibly the reason that people think that it was all about buildings is that we were initially more successful in getting funding from English Heritage, largely because it was the right moment. In the ten years or so that I was involved with the Project, one of the biggest problems was that funders were constantly changing their criteria. Someone takes over at the top of a funding agency and has a bright idea, so everything has to be "spun" to address that, and at the time building conservation was attracting funding. As it turned out this was a very good thing, because it allowed us to fill the gap in expertise at SDC – at a time before conservation officers were routinely employed by smaller local authorities.'

To their credit, SDC core-funded the Project, along with English Heritage; the Council contributed £20,000 towards annual core funding costs for the first three years. The money bought them a great deal of expertise, because Eddie Booth, English Heritage's Historic Area Adviser, was on the board and he was sufficiently high up in the hierarchy of English Heritage to be listened to. 'And we were very lucky with our first Project Officer, Chris Smith,' continues Mike. 'Chris had worked on various conservation projects; his job at the time was Conservation Officer for Avon, and he was also chair of the Association of Conservation Officers. He knew the legislation backwards and he was smart. So it changed the game, really. Instead of SDC being a backwoods council with no easy access to all of that, the Project was suddenly able to provide them with a lot of expertise.'

Chris Smith joined SVP in 1989 when he was phoned by Anne Mackintosh on the recommendation of Gordon Michell, and he moved to Stroud with his family from Bristol. Chris set up some standard procedures and became, with the encouragement of the Council, the person who regularly reviewed all the work of the planning department. 'Chris became an adjunct of the Council in that sense, but not controlled by them,' says Mike, 'and that meant we also had the benefit of his advice when it came to things that SDC were doing that we were not very keen on.' Every Monday morning he read the list of planning applications and identified the ones that SVP might want to have a view about. Chris's background was in planning departments. He remembers some big planning issues when he started: 'There was a Chief Planning Officer who had

Top: Chris Smith (left) welcoming Stroud Valleys Project patron, HRH Prince Michael of Kent
Bottom: The opening of the Georgian Bridge at Lodgemore Mill, 1993

strong views – as many professionals do – about him and his people being the right people to run all the planning services, but there were not many occasions on which his views were congruent with the community's. That came to a head in a number of very significant cases – the fight for the George in Nailsworth and other things.'

Chris found that his position as a professional interface made a big difference: 'I'd worked in local government and I didn't find it difficult to walk in and talk to people in the local authority in ways that I could make them feel comfortable when I needed to. And I could give them a new negotiating stance, which was something we consciously exploited.'

Building up relationships with councillors became an important part of the job too. Those on the Council who wanted to think the Project was right but needed new ammunition to use were able to quote a report written by a professional like Chris, who in turn had the back-up of English Heritage, and that became a potent way of starting to influence the broader picture.

'There's a whole list of projects that were done,' says Mike, 'some of them cosmetic improvements like the Georgian Bridge at Lodgemore Mill, others more strategic, like our input into the Area of Outstanding Natural Beauty revisions and the Local Plan. One project that is probably my favourite – and certainly gets lots of use all the time – is the walk along the banks of the Frome, replacing the canal towpath that had been lost when they put in the east-west bypass. I'm interested in community empowerment and the planning process, so setting up SVP was the important thing at that particular moment, and I think it undoubtedly saved us from the excesses of poorly controlled development that we would otherwise have suffered.'

When the first boundaries of the Cotswold AONB were drawn in the '60s, the boundary followed the Cotswold escarpment down into the back of Stroud and straight back out into what was thought of as 'proper countryside', excluding the mills. It was SVP who argued that the mills were important and should be included. 'Again, that was the trick – campaigning for that is one thing, but having a professional who's worked with professionals in cognate fields and can talk their language is even better,' says Chris. 'So we could play it both ways. While John Marjoram or David Drew (District Councillors) were going on about it on one side, it was quite handy to have someone go round the other side and talk from a professional level and say, let's look at the complex areas, you must agree this is a very out-of-date boundary.'

Some of the early and most effective things SVP did were to start to move the focus away from buildings. That was partly because there was already a good buildings trust in the Stroud valleys: the Stroud Preservation Trust. People began to realise that you could do more with less money by focusing on green projects, and this was in fact the path that SVP ended up following in the years to come.

By the time Chris moved on after six years in order to work for English Heritage, SVP had increased its profile and influence: 'I think what was good was the fact that we did empower campaigning,' he says. 'We reached the stage where I think most people had as much or more respect for the Project's view about planning policies and planning initiatives and individual planning casework in the Stroud Valleys as they did for the Council. And often there were councillors who would quote our advice rather than the advice of their own officers, and that was obviously professionally rewarding. But it was also great that you were actually doing what the idea was originally, which was to empower the Project and to turn its much better local knowledge into a currency that would achieve the objective.'

After Chris's departure, Caroline Aistrop was taken on in 1995 alongside Jagdish Patel, who was Project Coordinator. Some pioneering energy work was carried out in partnership with Stroud District Council. Kaye Welfare, who was an Energy Efficiency Coordinator with SDC and later became a SVP trustee, worked in partnership with SVP volunteer Richard Hoggett on various energy projects over

Bluebell walk in Randwick Woods with people with a visual impairment

'When I first started at the Council, it was quite unusual to have an Energy Efficiency Officer. It was ground-breaking to actually get these community energy projects together and get people thinking about saving energy, energy efficiency and renewable energy. At the time, there wasn't as much going on within the country,' says Kaye.

In partnership with Vision 21 (Energy 21 then) and SVP, Kaye set up one of the first solar clubs in the country where she brought together people to build their own DIY thermo-solar installation. 'That was the three organisations working together and in partnership, and it worked really well,' she says.

Another project, Enviromania, brought together all the local schools and took them to the District Council for a day, to look at different environmental aspects. And the Clean Energy Classroom was another success. Kaye explains: 'The Clean Energy Classroom was something that Stroud Valleys Project developed themselves. It was a fantastic little caravan classroom with computers in it and it had a little windmill and a PV panel, and they used to take it round to the schools and do events there. At the time, very little was known about renewables; they were seen as technologies that were quite different, when actually the classroom was trying to show that they were everyday technologies that could be used in all sorts of different places.'

Kaye, who now works at Severn Wye Energy Agency, feels the energy projects definitely had an impact: 'It certainly highlighted energy issues and the need to save energy, and the fact that there are a lot of people living in cold, damp homes and their health is affected by being in fuel poverty.'

Caroline Aistrop started working at SVP as a Countryside Management Officer. With a background in wildlife, her skills were around conservation and biodiversity. She inherited a number of projects that had volunteer community groups associated with them, like Dunkirk Mills Pond Group, the Roxborough House community garden, Brimscombe Wildlife Group, the Lake at the Lawns project and the Hamwell Leaze project. This 'green' work was seen by Stroud Valleys Project trustees as a way of getting the community involved: they could plant trees, put in steps, sow wildflower seeds – things that were easy for people to pick up. Then she developed a number of other projects, including forming the Bowbridge Canal Group which restored the mill pond near Arundel Mill, and getting involved in Stonehouse Newt Pond and monitoring the population of great crested newts. Later she ran adult education courses in a number of parishes and from one of those courses the Cainscross Wildlife Group was formed – a group of residents who looked after the local wildlife and created a wildlife map of the parish. The same was done in Cam, but on a larger scale. A parish map was created and special waymarked walks were made in the parish for people to follow. SVP did a survey showing that Cam residents valued their green spaces just as much as the countryside.

'Two really good sites came out of the Cam project,' says Caroline. 'One was Holywell Orchard, formerly an old orchard. We worked with local people to restore it, plant some apple and pear trees, and put a new bridge and footpath in. A theatre company came in and worked with local residents to create a play about the site, which was then performed one Easter, when the blossom was on the fruit trees.'

The other was the land in the middle of Cam, behind the Co-op (now Tesco). SVP arranged for an ecologist to survey the site, and he discovered that the site was actually a relic of what's called 'neutral grassland', now a very rare habitat. There are only five remaining sites of this type of habitat left in Gloucestershire; it's characteristic on the flat land that runs alongside rivers, and it was managed as hay meadow at one time. Eventually SVP got a 25-year lease from the Co-op, and they started working with local people to manage it. It's now flourishing – somebody does ecological surveys of it at regular intervals, a boardwalk has been put in, otter holts have been built, and there are interpretation boards in the car park.

The Severn Vale biodiversity project was another important project. The idea was to start rolling out what SVP had done in Cam to other parishes, but in a way that connected Cam up so that a wildlife corridor network could be developed and spread outwards. SVP did this work in partnership with Severnside Project, which was a project run by Gloucester City Council doing similar work. 'We got a lot of parishes involved,' says Caroline, 'there were 17 farmers around the area involved (including the Farming and Wildlife Advisory Group) and we got schools involved, and it was really beginning to make progress – until we hit a funding problem! And we had to say to the farmers, sorry, we can't continue to work with you, and once you've backed off it just kills all the enthusiasm, which is a great shame.'

Caroline then got involved in the Community Planning Conference, Energy 21 and the Farmers' Market, when Clare Gerbrands was based with SVP for the first year. 'I think that's one of the valuable roles of Stroud Valleys Project, which you can see with Energy 21, the Community Planning Conference and also something called the Stroud Community Land Trust [which takes on the lease or ownership of green spaces and works with SVP to do the practical work] – that we can provide support and a base to help people develop their ideas and projects,' says Caroline.

More recently, the emphasis of funders has moved towards working with people who are socially excluded and disadvantaged, and SVP got a grant to bring people with various disabilities, mental health or social problems into their work. They set up partnerships with Ruskin Mill and the Park House Day Centre for people with mental health problems. Caroline set up a project for people with visual impairment, bringing them into contact with wildlife. After she left, SVP went on to develop a programme with people with hearing disabilities as well. 'So actually we all found that work really quite rewarding,' says Caroline, 'which we hadn't expected to. It all seemed very big and scary to begin with, but the personal stories coming back on how much people had valued this type of involvement were very heartening.'

In the 13 years she was at SVP, Caroline saw funders' requirements change from accepting that you had to have core costs to pay for an office and overheads, to being much more project-focused. 'But you have to have staff in order to mobilise things,' she argues, 'and if you look at the number of volunteers we have and the amount of work that's happened, staff costs are tiny in comparison. The funders also have gone from seeming to accept that work needs to take quite a while for things to happen to wanting new and innovative things to happen all the time. And the paperwork's changed enormously. Within a few years, funders were demanding quarterly reports, detailed reports on all the funding that you'd spent, including copies of receipts for any expenses over £50, a detailed breakdown of your targets and how you were meeting them – to the point where we had to employ somebody to deal with the paperwork! You just lose the continuity and the Severn Vale biodiversity campaign was a classic example of that. You worked so hard to get other people motivated, enthusiastic, on board and doing things, and then you have to go and say, sorry.'

After being based in offices in John Street and then Kendrick Street, up four flights of stairs, SVP were keen to relocate to somewhere with a shop front. Initially they wanted a shop as an information centre, not necessarily to sell things. But then they realised that it could be dual purpose: they could try and get an income stream from it, and it could also act as an information point for people, which it does quite successfully. Information is now more accessible and people are on hand to answer questions. 'We think of that as a service to the community,' says Stella.

So what do the current trustees feel most proud of out of SVP's many achievements?

'It's about making things happen. The shop was one thing,' says Clare, 'and we were involved in setting up the Farmers' Market and that's made a huge difference to Stroud. And I'm also really proud of the Get Growing in Schools project, which we're doing at the moment, which is 23 schools setting up gardening clubs.'

'It's a question that's very hard to answer,' says Gerry, current chair of the trustees. 'We've done so many highly successful projects, which have had a real impact on communities in the Stroud area. When I look at some of the hedgerow projects, for example, in the Severn Vale, and the quality of the reports that have been produced on those – to me, for a small organisation like ours, it's astonishing. And they have had a tremendous permanent impact on wildlife in the Severn Vale.'

Geoff Beckerleg, another trustee, describes what attracted him to SVP: 'It's the variety of the projects really, because I don't think there's another charity that casts its net so wide. There are various specialist groups, but people who come to SVP can almost bring anything to the table.'

For the past three or four years SVP has focused on working with people with mental health problems and those recovering from drug and alcohol misuse. 'I think it's quite exciting that we've given people self-respect, the ability to have a social intercourse, inspire them with confidence,' says Gerry.

Clare points to the difficulties of attracting funding in this area, because improving people's wellbeing and confidence and self-esteem is a very difficult thing to quantify. 'But now we're finding much stronger ways of measuring it,' she says. 'I actually think that an easy measurement for us is the comments of the volunteers, and the obvious satisfaction they have from learning a new skill. And they're conscious themselves of the impact it's had on them,' adds Gerry.

'It's surprising really,' says Stella. 'Stroud is bang slap in the middle of a very beautiful area on the edge of an Area of Outstanding Natural Beauty, and yet quite a lot of people don't understand the area in which they live and why it's important. So, again, the strong thread is working with people. Over all these years we've done walks and talks, and tried to get people out, to look at, understand, and make a physical difference to where they're living and how they impact on the environment. And it's also about helping people in their local areas to appreciate and look after green spaces, rather than have urban cramming and filling everything up with housing – it's about how important green spaces are for wildlife and also for people's wellbeing.'

Interviewees: *Caroline Aistrop, Geoff Beckerleg, Mike Goodenough, Clare Mahdiyone, Stella Parkes, Gerry Robbins, Chris Smith, Kaye Welfare*

Opposite: Martin Large reviews the 'post-it' board in the CPC shop
Below: Stroud News & Journal open letter headline
Bottom: The precarious balancing act of the concerned citizen

Let's build the town that WE want

An open letter to
the people of
Stroud

5 The 1990s

The Community Planning Confererence (CPC) – 1995/6

'I loved the shop, especially a shop in the middle of town that is all about the town and which empowered people to come in and say what they thought they'd never say. Often they were not the kind of people who would have gone to council meetings, or a lot of them were too nervous to stand up in our big meetings and say something, so the fact that we had post-it notes and they could write down what they really thought – and they didn't have to put their names on it but it would count – that's what I think was really powerful about it.'

Stella Parkes, Organiser

ON 9 AUGUST 1995 A LETTER INITIATED by Alan Mossman appeared in the *Stroud News and Journal* entitled 'Let's build the town that WE want'. That letter stated that no comprehensive review or plan for Stroud town centre had been made since the saving of the High Street in the '70s; 32 shops were empty as were many significant buildings, including Blackboy's School, the Old Town Hall, an underused Subscription Rooms, the bingo hall and more. Parking and through traffic continued to irritate, the junior and infant school needed to merge, and so on. 'If we want a vibrant and sustainable town centre that is responsive to our needs we, all of us, can create it together'. That was the vision for a major community planning idea and the letter was signed by 30 people from local organisations and charities, traders, Stroud Town Council, the vicar, local businesses, and supported by the *Stroud News and Journal*.

The first meeting was scheduled for 16 August in St Lawrence Hall at 7.30, where people could come and talk about the idea, and discuss what could be done. Mike Goodenough remembers Alan 'visiting me in the garden; it was a lovely sunny afternoon and he sold me this line about what a good idea this would be. He approached a whole bunch of other people who he thought might carry some weight to put behind the idea of having a conference to address what we saw as the issue. There was something like 25% shop vacancy in the town and we wanted to discuss what we were going to do about that. The Council seemed to be asleep as usual.'

Alan had noticed a pattern in the campaigns of Stroud. 'I became aware that the pattern was the council propose and the town object and I wanted to do this a different way,' he says. The letter in the *SNJ* was the result of a month's whirlwind of talking to people all over town and in response to the District Council having produced a draft Local Plan that hadn't caught the imagination of many people.

150 people came to that initial meeting and every meeting from then on caught fire. Bill Hicks said that as local councillor and activist he was intrigued. He could see it was something different and he came to the conclusion that what was interesting was the fact that this was a community initiative and not the product of some form of officialdom or interest group.

The core committee that emerged over the next couple of months was engrossed in a process that took hours every week over the course of a year. The sum of £24,200 was raised from the District and Town Councils. This money supported the process, the conferences and the many meetings, and paid for a part-time co-ordinator employed through Stroud Valleys Project. Looking back over the 16 months of action, 1,180 days of volunteer time was donated and support in kind came from over 50 local organisations and businesses. Over 350 people came to the various meetings and conferences and thousands more contributed via the CPC shop.

Alan ran that first meeting on a hot August night and was overwhelmed by the response. His early undergraduate research and later work had used a process called 'charette' where large groups of people were involved in planning for their neighbourhoods. He had run this process successfully in Trafford Borough Council (part of Greater Manchester) – surely it would work in Stroud? Other people in the room also had their favourite methods. There was concern that it would be a 'battle of the professionals' rather than being very much community-led.

However, the talking had started and within a month there was a second public meeting with presentations from different methodologies: Planning for Real presented by John Colvin; cultural quarter and town planning from Nick Falk of Urbed, who had written the 'String of Pearls' report more than 10 years earlier that showed up the wonders of the Valleys' mills; Sue Porter, a consultant and Stroud local, and Alan Mossman once again outlining the idea for a Community Planning Conference.

The last idea was chosen by that audience because it seemed more organic and less structured than the others and could also be run by those who got involved, without a clear leadership and without experts running the show. The ideal was to allow different ideas to come to the surface. This wasn't an easy time, negotiating without clear leaders and thinking how best to run the whole project. Bill Hicks again: 'From an entirely personal point of view it was a very interesting learning curve. I mean, I'd spent four years on the District Council, which is a very adversarial, very often negative arena to participate in and the idea of proceeding on the basis of consensus and no votes, was, I have to say, a very attractive eye-opener for me. I think it did succeed remarkably well. The fact that you're dealing with planning issues, but also having an entire group looking at the sort of inherent community values, and the way you go about things, and in the things you're proposing, that too was very refreshing and an interesting experience.'

Gradually groups got together. A small team emerged to plan the February conference; others met weekly to keep the ball rolling, negotiate with the Councils and move on the project; and a major public meeting looked at values to underpin the work. Stroud Valleys Project became the umbrella organisation to deal with the finances and in the New Year of 1996 a shop was opened in Cornhill, 12 Union Street and called Up2Us. For that opening the CPC launched a New Year's Three Wishes. 'I can claim that idea,' says Stella Parkes. 'We gave everyone three post-it notes when they came in and said if you had three wishes for Stroud what would they be?' Over the weeks, 4,000 wishes were collected and many of the primary schools joined in as well.

Graphics poured from the pens and computers of designer Bill Hicks and Martin Sievey and the Three Wishes campaign was well supported by the *Stroud News and Journal*. Mike Goodenough remembers that the CPC got the shop partly because of such support from the *News and Journal*. 'They ran a weekly column and produced a map as a centre spread for the Three Wishes campaign. They were very keen to promote and debate what could be done. They were fully signed up to the idea of having this kind of open conversation where everybody got the opportunity to explain their point of view.'

There were concerns for those organising and planning the conference meeting – people argued endlessly about process. Mike Goodenough: 'I seem to remember one dreadful moment. I was in a committee that was devoted to process. I very nearly went out and hung myself.'

Somewhere in the mix Bill Hicks thought up the Furry Godfather in slippers and a tutu. The Furry Godfather arrived on the High Street and granted people their three wishes and then appeared on the pages of newsletters, news articles and CPC adverts and cartoons. Even a giant Santa hung out with passers-by near the Up2Us shop. It wasn't all 'process' with the CPC, it was a lot of hard work and fun as well.

The first conference was held at the Acorn Hall on Union Street on 2–4 February. Again, unprecedented numbers of people (220) came. Friday night was picturing the Stroud we wanted, Saturday was integrating everyone's wishes into the overall picture, developing the picture and key areas and forming fact-finding groups, and then Sunday was agreeing what we needed

The Furry Godfather grants wishes on the High Street (Stroud News & Journal)

THE CROSS

FAWKES PLACE

CIVIC SQUARE

Ideas for transforming Stroud's public spaces

to find out to enable us to prepare an action plan at the next conference, summarising and agreeing tasks.

Ten weeks later the second conference was to bring back all the research and ideas from the 26 groups formed in early February. Those ten weeks was really busy. The core groups covered such aspirations and concerns as arts, children, entertainment, governance, health, housing, recycling, town layout, trees and landscape, young people and values. Some of the smaller groups merged. Two more public meetings on the Future of Town Centres and Building on Stroud's Uniqueness again attracted debate and information. The Three Wishes campaign went on. A request for a beach seemed a good idea, and for solar-powered heating for the outdoor pool! Many of the school children wanted more flowers to stop Stroud being so dull. Nearly everyone wanted a cinema.

Thanks to the company 3M we were donated thousands of post-it notes, and we needed them as they were used for the 4,000 wishes and for all the meetings. Stella Parkes: 'I was working in Bristol at one point and I had done quality management training there using lots and lots of post-it notes, which seemed to me a really, really excellent way of getting ideas out of your head onto a piece of paper.' It was a new technique to many of us who were not management consultants and we really enjoyed it!

At the second conference on 12–14 April 1996 the project groups reported their ideas, their research and their vision for Stroud. There were 11 groups all developing action plans – arts, economic regeneration, housing, pedestrians, bikes and traffic, quality of the built environment, shops and streetlife, visitors and tourism, young people, trees and landscaping, and health. Behind these groups a big debate had been held at the first conference on what the principles were to abide by – there were so many. That there are always so many in Stroud reflects a thoughtful community wanting accessibility for all, sustainability, child-friendly streets, high quality services, local creativity to be prioritised, integrated transport planning and a positive image of Stroud, amongst many others.

The second conference was very difficult. Differences in opinion on how the first evening session was to be run resulted in a pretty public wrangle, but everyone worked together eventually to put together a Big Picture map, to look through the collated 4,000 wishes, and to bring together the different action plans of the groups.

What was it that the CPC was really trying to change?
Stella Parkes: 'The councils – getting the councils to listen and take us seriously, and to work in a co-productive way with us instead of just deciding what they thought was best for the district and not asking anybody else. So that was the challenge really – to make ourselves established enough so that they would start listening to what we were saying.'

Mike Goodenough: 'Well, my interest was to try and find some way to turn the dynamism of dissent and opposition into something positive and we tried to do that with the setting up of the Stroud Valleys Project, but it became clear very quickly that you couldn't do it within an organisation that had to have clear funded objectives. So I think, I naively thought, if we can do this – and having set up the Stroud Preservation Trust as well, there were two organisations that are doing these things on the ground – don't we all deserve to have a meaningful part in forming policy? Not in any way subverting the role of politicians, but to inform them. I mean my frustration is always that you make a presentation to politicians, but they've got other things on their minds and unless they have a really specific interest in what you're telling them they don't listen.'

Bill Hicks was particularly taken with the idea that the whole project proceeded on the basis of consensus. Also a plus for him was the fact that we had a non-partisan media. There were lots of people from different aspects of the community. 'Politically we had all three parties and the Greens, four parties, represented there, operating and discussing things at the same table with one another without having any need to toe the party line, or for any party whipping. The exciting things were the number of people, for example like Tim Mars, who came. And they gave most erudite deliveries, which meant I was learning something new practically every time we met. It raised consciousness.

Certainly I'd been on the planning committee for four years, but I know that an awful lot of people had no notion at all about planning and were learning about it as they were going along.'

Between the second conference and offering the report to the District Council in early July 1996 it was felt that the District Council wanted to take over from where the CPC had got to. They decided that they wanted to set up a town centre partnership. Mike Goodenough explains: 'Well, they also got some money – I can't remember where the money came from – it was broadly for urban regeneration. We felt that as we'd done all this work we were in a position to give some shake to that and curiously enough, the recommendation that we came up with was not for town centre management but for events management. We wanted to employ someone to make the best of not only Stroud but also Dursley by encouraging markets and so on; that's really where the Farmers' Market grew from.'

The CPC group meanwhile was writing a detailed bid for regeneration money, 'Developing a Positive Image for Stroud', that was targeted to significantly increase the town's footfall in the short term. This was turned down as premature by the District Council on 5 November 1996. The town centre manager idea had been decided on and it felt that all the CPC work was being rejected. The CPC had put in a wealth of ideas and action plans for the town but this wasn't a strategy – although the CPC thought it was. The footfall proposal certainly was a strategy but the District Council decided on its own path and in November 1996 exhausted volunteers were deflated.

The November 1996 CPC Newsletter No. 3 was entitled 'Damp Squib for Stroud'.

In that newsletter Mike Goodenough wrote: 'The result of a year's listening, discussing and research was dismissed as 'premature' by Stroud District Council's Planning Committee on 5 November. There was no debate, no response to the detailed points that CPC had raised and, worst of all, no attempt to grapple with what the 'regeneration' of Stroud might actually involve. CPC's

CPC NEWSLETTER

Published by Stroud Community Planning Conference
12 Union Street, Stroud • Telephone 01453 766422

ISSUE 3
November 1996

EDITORIAL STATEMENT

STROUD COMMUNITY PLANNING CONFERENCE is a forum, open to all, in which people express a variety of views and work together with the common aim of restoring economic prosperity and vitality to the quality of life in our community.

CPC has no party political alignment nor any manifesto. People from all the political groups in local politics can be found in CPC working groups alongside many with no political loyalties.

The views expressed in this newsletter are those of the contributors and are not necessarily shared by CPC as a whole. CPC has the declared aim of gathering information and encouraging debate and participation of the public in planning issues. The editors intend that this newsletter will be increasingly effective in involving people, airing all views and uncovering facts and fabrications without fear or favour.

EDITORIAL TEAM FOR NOVEMBER ISSUE

Chris Free, Bill Hicks, Stella Parkes & Sue Porter

PLEASE SEND LETTERS AND ARTICLES FOR PUBLICATION AND OFFERS OF HELP WITH NEWSLETTER PRODUCTION TO CPC SHOP 12 UNION STREET

DAMP SQUIB FOR STROUD

Reporter: Mike Goodenough

The result of a year's listening, discussion and research was dismissed as "premature" by Stroud District Council's Planning Committee on November 5th.

Anyone expecting fireworks would, however, have been disappointed. Cllr John Marjoram let off a "Smack in the face for Stroud" and a couple of "Disappointed and angry"s, but to no avail. New Labour had made up its collective mind. There was no debate, no response to the detailed points CPC had raised, and, worst of all, no attempt to grapple with what the 'regeneration' of Stroud might actually involve.

CPC's widely supported Regeneration Fund bid had set out a short-term strategy to address this. Based on the conclusion that the window dressing of environmental improvements would not in itself achieve any significant change in Stroud's fortunes; the Promotions Manager element of the bid had always been seen as critical to its success.

To dismiss the Promotions Manager as "premature", despite the fact that the post would have neither preempted the work of the Town Centre Partnership nor anticipated town centre management, seems to me to completely miss the point.

• Inside: Sue Porter on Brick Row • Chris Free on Planning •

The November 1996 CPC Newsletter No. 3

widely supported Regeneration Fund bid had set out a short term strategy to address this. Based on the conclusion that window dressing or environmental improvements would not in themselves achieve any significant change in Stroud's fortunes, the Promotions Manager element of the bid had always been seen as critical to its success. To dismiss the Promotions Manager as 'premature' despite the fact that the post would have neither pre-empted nor anticipated town centre management seems to me to completely miss the point.'

What did come out of that process, those 16 months of meetings, inspiration, conversation and ideas? Was the CPC a catalyst? It certainly felt so. The debate had been had. The will was there to support new ideas in the community and people went off to make things happen. The District Council's initial rejection of the CPC report was disappointing but SDC made things happen too – many of which had been discussed during those heated conferences. The Town Centre Partnership had two people on its committee from the CPC carrying forward the ideas raised.

The Farmers' Market emerged with the energy of Clare Gerbrands and the support of Stroud Valleys Project.

An arts quarter? Neil Walker and Jo Leahy were there in those early CPC days. They came to Stroud to set up an artists' studio space and with the support of Peter Batemen, local landlord and owner of the Bateman's sports shop, that is what they did. In the past 17 years Stroud Valleys Artspace have set up Open Studios, the artists' studios building and the SITE Festival. The arts group continued on for at least a year after CPC's second conference.

The Subscription Rooms were revamped in late 1996 with appointed architects in close links with the CPC arts group. It has taken time but is now buzzing with activities and is much more closely linked into other festivals and events. The British School hall has lately been restructured as a theatre. New professional theatre companies have set up.

Lansdown Hall and Gallery is owned and used by the community for arts in the gallery and other events. The Stroud International Textile Festival brings textile workers from far afield. Stroudwater Textile Trust (established in 2000) merges textile techniques with the history and machinery of the mills. SVA have taken on the Goods Shed as a major new arts venue. The gallery at Stroud Museum in the Park offers a constant stream of dynamic exhibitions featuring mainly Stroud Valleys artists. The Museum itself is a success story of regeneration, moving into the park in 2001. The cinema was built at Merrywalks in 2004 (the old cinema could not be acquired by the cinema group for the community and is a dance hall now). There is a bowling alley as well.

The night-time economy was talked about. During the time of the CPC there were around five cafés in Stroud; now there are nearly 30. There are more restaurants opening and established, some in this last serious recession. The shops went through a phase of nearly being full. Anne Mackintosh still runs the shop windows project where she negotiates as many empty shop windows as possible for displays and exhibitions of local groups. The health group run by Alice Windsor and Sue Porter developed into a District-wide forum and met regularly for over four years.

Was it worth all the effort?

Mike Goodenough: 'Yes, it was worth doing, it was worth doing. For me the core benefit would have been to find some way to create some sort of dynamic contact with the local authorities – it's always worth the exercise. We all certainly learned a great deal.'

Stella Parkes: 'I loved the shop, especially a shop in the middle of town that is all about the town and which empowered people to come in and say what they thought they'd never say. Often they were not the kind of people who would have gone to council meetings, or a lot of them were too nervous to stand up in our big meetings and say something, so the fact that we had post-it notes and they could write down what they really thought – and they didn't have to put their names on it but it would count – that's what I think was really powerful about it.'

'Yes it was great,' continues Mike. 'And surprising people too, putting all those huge and ridiculous posters up. It made people laugh a lot, I think, which was good.'

Bill Hicks: 'I met all sorts of people that possibly one wouldn't. Yes, it's an excellent thing to do for one's physical and mental health. Active citizenship is great, it ought to be compulsory really. It also added to the critical mass which is both Stroud's self image and also its public image of being a community which is proactive, that does have movers and shakers in spades, and is not to be messed about with frankly.'

'It's time to do it again, isn't it?' says Stella. 'How about an exhibition, the Three Wishes campaign once more, and another go at a truly community-inspired neighbourhood planning process! Stroud is still stroppy – it should work!'

Interviewees: *Mike Goodenough, Stella Parkes, Bill Hicks, Alan Mossman*

People who were involved in the whole CPC process:
(and apologies to the many who contributed that we have not listed)
Alan Mossman, Mike Goodenough, Stella Parkes, Anne Mackintosh, Nick Falk, Camilla Hale, Martin Sievey, Sue Porter, Martin Quick, Fiona Ellis, Dave Cockcroft, John Marjoram, David Drew, Martin Harwood, Caroline Aistrop, Clive Miller, Ken Hall, Joe Seex, Rev Father Barry, Rob Green, Lesley Green, Carol Kambites, Julia Bennett, Bill Hicks, Tom Medcalf, Andrew Watton, Bill Wrather (Merrywalks owner), Chris Free, Alice Windsor, Jacky Martel, Shelagh Jones, John Mills, Maggie Mills, Mr and Mrs Hopwood, Jenny Bailey, Glen Hall, Tim Mars, Charles Landry.

6 The Farmers' Market 1999

The 1990s

'The Farmers' Market came at the right time – everyone wanted a big community event that was going to bring everyone together and yes, it just hit the right note.'

Gerb Gerbrands

'Stroud embraced the food movement wholeheartedly with its sense of the importance of the local, of community and of organics. It is a small enough town to embrace an idea, but large enough to sustain it.'

Clare Honeyfield

STROUD FARMERS' MARKET HAS BEEN a most wonderful thing for Stroud. Dynamic, economically viable and award-winning, it seemed just to leap into being. The town is proud of its market. Visitors come from all over the UK and the world to visit; every Saturday there is a hum of anticipation and enjoyment in Cornhill. How did this happen?

Clare Gerbrands (now Honeyfield) was the engine behind the Farmers' Market but she started her market expertise years before when she set up the Made in Stroud craft markets. Clare's then husband Kardien Gerbrands (Gerb) was making tongue drums and they were selling them through craft markets and schools workshops. Clare remembers: 'We were spending a lot of time at these craft markets and spending money on travel and stall rental and I wondered if we could do something more cost-effective. There was no craft market in our area then and so I started a weekday seasonal market in St Laurence Hall and there were 37 stalls of local makers at that first market. It was great for me – I had a one-year-old, two-year-old and four-year-old and I thought it would be nice to have an interest outside of the home.'

Clare had developed a lot of skills organising events through her teens in Churchdown for the Scouts – she wrote press releases, arranged events, raised money and generally knew that 'in the community it was possible to make anything happen'.

Gerb got involved in community activism in his teens through Starters Café in the High Street at the end of the '70s – a time, he says, when alternative views were emerging and flourishing in Stroud. Friends of the Earth, tai chi, meditation – everything was becoming open and available, new people were moving into town and recognising the value of the place and its beauty. It was important for him to observe the impact of the High Street and Ring Road campaigns and the way in which they were won. Fighting for the trees in Stratford Park was another community success. He felt that Stroud was not valued in the '70s but gradually a sense of itself emerged.

These early markets were built on Clare doing all the networking through personal contacts, mostly on Friday mornings at The Shambles market. Discussing the first market coined the name. 'Artist Alice Friend said of course it must be called Made in Stroud because that is what it is!' says Clare. The markets were really successful and later moved into the Subscription Rooms.

'It was always about community action and the sharing of ideas,' says Clare, 'not about me personally. In the Subscription Rooms I met Isabella Blow and she was really interested in the idea of Cotswold makers – we talked through a lot of ideas and others wanted me to start a shop, but I didn't want to sit in a shop all the time. In 1992/3 Gerb and I went travelling around Italy and Spain busking in the markets and I noticed women with just a bucket of lemons and people selling home-grown produce – we had a real and direct relationship with the countryside then.'

Both Clare and Gerb were part of the Community Planning Conference and there was a lot of talk about markets and how they could revitalise the town and the idea of Made in Stroud. At a meeting with Stroud District Council Clare negotiated a grant to trial the idea of a market using the District Council-built Cornhill. That grant had been allocated to a market feasibility study but Clare advocated community action – starting a market using local food producers was a better way to test the water than merely doing the research. Clare's cuttings from the craft markets sold the idea to Alan Caig, the then Arts and Sports development officer for Stroud District Council. He asked Clare to come back to him with a budget and an outline business plan. Alan also told Clare about Gloucestershire Food Links and working with farmers, and how important that would be for the market. Clare as a vegetarian had quite strong and pretty negative views about farmers but took on board the advice.

Jo Leahy and Neil Walker had recently started Stroud Valleys Artspace and they helped Clare with that initial budget and talked through publicity ideas as well. 'When I typed up the budget for the first year on my typewriter on my kitchen table it came to £6,500 and I thought I can't possibly ask for that much. However, I posted it to the council and then had another meeting, this time with three officers, and they said that I had done a lovely job but I hadn't paid myself anything so they would give me £10,000!'

Because the money had to go through a charity, Stroud Valleys Project was approached by SDC and Clare set up there with a desk, computer training, strategic planning and volunteer support time. She was based at Stroud Valleys Project for about 15 months from early 1999.

Before Cornhill was built there had been a successful street market in Union Street run by marketeers from the Midlands, but once Cornhill was available seemingly nothing worked there except as a venue for the Fringe Festival. Some local people arranged to do a spiritual cleansing before the first Farmers' Market and advised on the colour of flowers and other things to ensure the market was a success. Later on Stroud Valleys Artspace built the railings so that metal fencing wasn't needed for every event. These were examples of where community came to the Farmers' Market and added to it, rather than always being initiated by Clare.

The volunteer worker at SVP rang all the farmers in the area. Most of them thought that they had nothing to sell and that people would not be interested in their produce. The first people interested were Frocester Fayre – they only wanted half a stall to begin with. Now they have a farm shop, a cutting centre for other farmers and they attend about 14 markets a month.

Clare was never short of brilliant ideas, networks and energy. She researched the movement and the rules of Farmers' Markets – the absolute link to localism, food miles and good products. She linked into the national movement. Robert Rees approached Clare to cook in the market each week. He was passionate about good food for everyone and Stroud Town Council stepped in to pay for the cooking equipment. It was Clare's focus – obsession, even – that got the whole thing going; she set up the business and organised the funding.

Stroud's Farmers' Market leapt off the page straight away in July of 1999; it was at the forefront of the new interest in food in Britain. There was real gloss on that first day with celebrities Jasper Conran and Isabella Blow from the fashion world opening this first Farmers' Market in Gloucestershire (and only the third in England). It was a glamorous and dynamic opening and it immediately raised the profile of Stroud.

Almost every year since that triumphant opening the Stroud Farmers' Market has won awards: 'Hero of Gloucestershire' in 2000 (Clare); Cotswolds Food and Drink Best Farmers' Market 2003 and 2004; the most sustainable business 'Eat the View' national award in 2005; Radio 4's Food and Farming Awards, Best Farmers' Market in 2008 and 2010; and Farmers' Market of the Year from FARMA in 2013. This is just a sample of the awards.

Clare immediately got involved with the detail of how a Farmers' Market could be run – there was no guidance and no national standard. Joining representatives from the Farmers' Union, the Farm Retail Association and the Soil Association, she says, 'We set up the National Association of Farmers' Markets based at Evolve in Bath. We set up a sub-committee which I sat on for two years and looked into the minutiae of how do we choose who comes to the markets? We decided to give first choice to organic but we had to work through all the questions: what is the definition of local, what about the WI and what about plants and marmalade? The standard that we developed became adopted as the national standard. I also wrote a criteria for craft markets which has also become a national standard.

'We got DEFRA funding for three years to start with to write a set of food safety criteria for Farmers' Markets. We did this with Gloucestershire Trading Standards and the Food Safety Group. That set of criteria have also been adopted as national standards.'

Originally conceived as a co-operative with the producers, the farmers then decided that they wanted to concentrate on what they were good at and that Clare should go ahead and set it all up as a business. Stroud District Council supported the move – they were keen to see the market self-supporting within three years. 'So I set up Made in Stroud Ltd with Gerb as the co-director. He was helping with the paperwork and finances then, which was never my strong point.'

To start with, the Farmers' Markets were set up with producers coming from a 30-mile radius. This has now been extended to 50 miles. To run a premium market like Stroud it has to be full and with a waiting list of producers wanting to come on board. Gerb explains: 'The whole concept of Farmers' Markets – the push behind it, if you like, the energy – came from a desperate need within farming, especially for small family-sized farms, to be able to continue trading and get a realistic price for their produce, because they were being pushed out of wholesale markets by the demands of supermarkets.' Within a few miles of Stroud there are very few vegetable producers who can deliver week after week – Stroud is lucky enough to have three really local vegetable producers and local cheese and meat producers. Many other places can hardly get that standard within 30 or even 50 miles. The London Farmers' Markets have a radius of 100 miles because the city itself takes up so much area.

Clare and Gerb also developed other Farmers' Markets in Dursley and

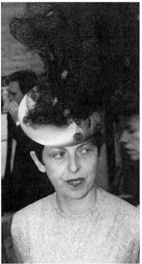

Top: Launching the Farmers' Market (left) Jasper Conran with Clare Gerbrands, (right) Isabella Blow
Below: David Drew MP at the launch

Nailsworth, in Cirencester and in Stow. Through 2000 the Stroud market ran twice a month, as did Cirencester's.

Stroud District Council recorded the changes in footfall for Saturdays in Stroud and noted that footfall increased throughout the town, not just around the market. The economic changes were seen from very early on. Some stallholders were at the end of their tether as producers and were about to give up. Other traders had to have full-time jobs but gradually were able to sell and develop their business so that they could concentrate full-time on being producers. Others found the markets gave them opportunities to sell fruit damaged by hail – perfectly sound fruit not accepted by the supermarkets but sold through Farmers' Markets direct to the customer.

The energy that Clare and Gerb put into those early years is amazing. 'We always had our fingers in something else!' They started Stow once a month – a tiny, lovely market which they still run. They were invited to Gloucester to set up a weekly Friday market and ran that for nine years. They tried Lechlade for a while, Malmesbury for three years and now run one at the Designers Outlet in Swindon.

The DEFRA grant also supported training for producers on how to enter into direct selling: what was needed for dairy, meat, vegetables and eggs. Workshops were run around the county and the plan was that all the Farmers' Markets would be certified by FARMA (National Farmers' Retail and Markets Association). Guidelines were drawn up, health and safety and insurance information given, an application pack for producers developed, Farmers' Market rules and conditions were printed as well as a marketing leaflet for all the markets in the county.

Tensions started arising between the Farmers' Market trend and other large-scale general market managers and the success of Stroud and Clare made others envious and divisive. The programme didn't run the full three years – the leaflet idea was offered to others but division, suspicion and jealousies broke down the whole county intention.

Clare and Gerb continued to be involved in wider projects but it was not easy. There were a couple of years of running all kinds of food programmes in the Forest of Dean, Apple Days, school visits to farms, workshops for farms on how to have farm visits and developing guidelines for education visits. The funding for this work came from Gloucestershire Food Links for a limited time, but then other organisations changed the focus of the work and quite quickly the project came to a halt.

Even after these two hard lessons about the perils of public funding and territorial difficulties, Gerb was involved in a local, fresh food sourcing project for schools. It seemed such a simple issue – find out what's needed, look at nutritional content, find local producers and ensure that schools get that produce. After 18 months of meetings and little action, a contract went out for fruit for schools through a major Bristol fruit importer. 'It was pretty disillusioning!' says Gerb.

Clare and Gerb decided to concentrate on their business and not be involved in grant or public funding projects again. They were working full-time and needed to pull back from such a huge agenda. 'When you are working with funding,' says Clare, 'about a third of your time is taken up with applying for the funding and about a third of your time is spent reporting. So if you are passionate about the projects you then do even more to make it all happen. It also became important to us to stay with projects that are sustainable financially.'

Only 15 months after launching the Stroud Farmers' Market, Clare and Gerb opened the Made in Stroud shop at the Goodwill Evening in December 2000. This seemed a logical extension of their earlier craft markets and of the increasing demand for crafts to be sold through the Farmers' Market. The Made in Stroud name was very important to them – it had been the name for their quarterly craft markets a decade earlier and Clare made sure that it was fully owned by them. The Made in Stroud shop is in a building where a local owner had brought the building back into full use, with offices and flats upstairs, a lovely shop on the street and a local business occupying the shop – win win all round. The shop offered a town centre information point for the Farmers'

Farmers' Market producers

Market run by Clare, and an office base for the Made in Stroud initiative as well as the shop, run by Gerb. There was no longer a need to be based at Stroud Valleys Project.

Initially the Made in Stroud shop was a co-op. Everyone who sold crafts, jewellery, cards, pottery and so on had to work in the shop so there was no staff outlay, nil pounds at the outset and around £50 profit or something at the end of the first year. As long as everything was being paid, that was fine. Everyone brought in their own bags, and no money was spent that wasn't there to spend.

Six years later Clare and Gerb set up the Made in Gloucestershire shop in Westgate, Gloucester. They were in a South West Regional Development shop and borrowed money to set up the shop with all the packaging and tools needed to run a six-day-a-week premises. Staff was needed (the Stroud shop and the markets took up an enormous amount of their time). They sold more in terms of volume in Gloucester than in Stroud, but with the debt and then the owners wanting a threefold rent raise, they knew they could not continue the Gloucester shop after the initial three years.

All the projects and businesses that Clare and Gerb have been involved in over the past 14 years have needed constant assessment and change, especially as so much of their work has been trailblazing and innovative.

The Made in Stroud shop had reached a ceiling turnover and some craft workers only 'owed' a day or two a year of working in the shop. The amount of training needed for temporary shop running meant that more and more time was demanded of Clare and Gerb to ensure that everything went well and that finances were overseen thoroughly. 'We could never switch off,' says Gerb. He explains the next moves: 'We had a committee and we couldn't get the changes needed to raise the turnover, so we offered to take over the company, turn it into a community interest company, increase the percentage commission, remove the need to work in the shop and employ a shop manager.' Some of the craft workers left as they didn't want things to go this way, but the

Karen Debonnaire conducts the Stroud Community Choir at the Farmers' Market launch

shop has thrived. It is now fully owned by Clare and is a major retail enterprise in the town.

The Farmers' Market has also changed. At the start Gerb and Clare would know 95% of the people shopping. Now it's more like 15%. There are more people there but less is spent than in the early days. There are Community-supported Agriculture projects now, more farm shops, local food in the supermarkets, and doorstep organic veg deliveries through the UK. However, the fame of the Stroud Market has travelled. People come from London and Manchester; the Portishead Friendly Circle came for a day out, and people have visited from Japan.

The markets are all on contracts. Despite starting out with a grant from Stroud District Council the Farmers' Market now pays annual rent and is on a three-year contract which has to be renegotiated. More change came after nine years of running the Gloucester market – they lost the contract to a large organisation.

Since March 2013 Gerb now owns and runs the Farmers' Markets business and Clare's ownership is now fully with the Made in Stroud shop. Reflecting on the various projects they have been involved in, Gerb says, 'Clare's drive was there right from the beginning. She joined the national FARMA's board; she negotiated the DEFRA grant; she developed the protocols on how a Farmers' Market should be run and was relentless in her pursuit of press coverage. It was adventurous and we were full of hope. I think that the Farmers' Market links back to the whole thing about Starters Café. Stroud was embracing alternative ideas on the High Street and it seemed like it inspired a whole generation and attracted in people with similar values and ideas to the town. The Farmers' Market came at the right time – everyone wanted a big community event that was going to bring everyone together and yes, it just hit the right note.' Clare feels that 'Stroud embraced the food movement wholeheartedly with its sense of the importance of the local, of community and of organics. It is a small enough town to embrace an idea, but large enough to sustain it.'

And as Clare also looks back over the last 15 exciting years she is sad not to be able to share it all with Isabella Blow, who had such a clear vision of the potential of the crafts markets and the food market. Isabella died in 2007 and Clare would have loved her to continue as mentor and inspiration.

Interviewees: *Clare Honeyfield, Kardien Gerbrands*

Below: Flies on the Wall youth theatre production
Bottom: Lansdown Hall hosts the Stroud Fringe Festival in Bank Gardens

7 The Space, Lansdown Hall & Gallery – 1999

The 1990s

'I think what I'm pleased about is that people now come and have a good experience; it's brought everything together. We've been able to improve the facilities for a lot of different users – you've got yoga people who want it quiet and warm and zumba people who want it bright and loud, so everything we do has got flexibility in it. We want as much flexibility as possible. We seem to have managed to achieve that – all the user groups are happy.'

Jeremy Collingwood

Chair of Trustees, Lansdown Hall & Gallery

'I THINK IN TERMS OF COMMUNITY

and community action, the fact that Stroud Common Wealth bought the building was really important to start with,' says Lansdown Hall & Gallery trustee Jo Bousfield. 'And I think that where it is placed geographically is really important. It's right in the middle of the town. It's not like the Sub Rooms, it's not like SVA, it's not like the Cotswold Playhouse. It really feels like a huge village hall with nice resources that people are familiar with.'

'Whatever the event or celebration, it just feels like the right kind of space,' adds administrator Sue Bearder.

Since the 1880s Lansdown Hall has been through many guises – built originally as a temperance hall it has been a Christian Science church, a museum, a soft ball play area. It was finally put up for the sale in 1999 by the then owners, Gloucestershire County Council and was bought for £112,000 by Stroud Common Wealth for use as a community arts centre. A group of people led by

Martin Large and Lucas Shoemaker set up Stroud Common Wealth as a not-for-profit company limited by guarantee; its original strapline was 'For Cultural, Social and Economic Renewal'. When he was chair of Shire Training Workshops, Martin had started up a part-time Foundation Course in Art, based at the British School, followed soon after by a Foundation Course in Drama, where three drama teachers and 100 part-time drama students produced six to eight plays every year. This performing arts course needed a home, so when the Hall came up for sale, Martin asked a number of drama groups and performing arts groups whether they would use the place. The answer was yes, so he led a campaign for its purchase with the support of Labour MP David Drew. A mortgage was obtained from the Midland Bank and money was raised by public subscription, with people giving interest-free loans or gifts.

But the relationship with the County Council was difficult. 'It's a story of civil society and the community trying to work constructively with a reluctant statutory sector,' says Martin. 'Gloucestershire County Council had their lawyers put in various clauses that we couldn't lease Lansdown Hall to any other body for longer than five years, which made it very difficult for anybody we were leasing to to get a mortgage or grant to renew the place. The GCC Property and Estates people wanted money and they refused to realise they've also got a cultural and social economic set of policies. So that made it quite difficult.' But despite these potential difficulties for the future, Stroud Common Wealth went ahead and bought it. 'We had £5,000 in the kitty and our plan was always to secure the asset and then lease it or rent it to a charitable arts charity that would run it.'

'I remember the first night we were there,' continues Martin. 'We facilitated the evening. There were 72 people there, I think, there was candlelight, lanterns, very dim lights. The acoustics were terrible and we thought, oh my God, will it fly as a venue, because the acoustics were so appalling? You had to shout to be heard. But it went brilliantly and we coined the name The Space – Stroud Performing Arts Centre. Jo Bousfield, formerly of Dr Fosters and now of Flies on the Wall, said, 'The community needs a dance floor to dance on.'

The Town Council supported the project, but not the District. Martin recalls being told by various arts administrators that it wouldn't work. 'I remember a Green councillor coming along and telling us that the statistics show that there aren't audiences. But in fact the audiences were very good and it went very well. All sorts of groups like Dr Foster's, Flies on the Wall, Company of Friends, Dramarama, visiting companies and Commedia dell'Arte groups – it soon filled up with fantastic things and was a success in those terms, but took a huge amount of work getting going. I can remember running a cabaret once a month with four or five different groups on a Friday and I was washing all the glasses till late at night. We pulled in £300 or £400 a month just for that, so it made a difference.'

Sue Bearder, who had been so involved in re inventing the Fringe Festival, joined the Space as an employee of the charity (now called Stroud's Art Centre, trading as Lansdown Hall & Gallery). 'That was very refreshing, because she knew how to run it!' says Martin. Then, after unsuccessfully approaching the Town Council several times as a possible purchaser, Stroud Common Wealth sold the building for the same price as it was bought for, to arts charity Reclaim Arts. 'We at Stroud Common Wealth didn't want to run it any more; our job is to enable the development of social and cultural enterprises and we had other things to do,' says Martin.

Jo explains: 'Reclaim Arts was a charity that a woman had set up at the British School at Painswick Inn and it was all about recycled arts. When she moved to London, the charity was just sitting there, so she offered it to The Space, which was very useful as we needed to be a charity and we were able to just take over the charity 'shell' for free.

'I was Chair of the Trustees for several years. My heart is absolutely in community, I think it's the reason for life, really – to be in a place where you know everyone and there's all that interaction. I'm not a city, anonymous person at all. So I chaired it because I was the only person around really. But I wasn't very proactive, and since Jeremy arrived, thank goodness, and Stroud Town Council bought it, it's all got back into shape.'

The pool of volunteers at The Space was tiny. There were different fund-raising schemes for the building, including a campaign where you could get your name on a brick if you contributed financially. 'Money would trickle in but that was just plugging a hole and we couldn't then do what we wanted to do,' Jo says. 'The state of the building meant that we couldn't really up our charges because the loos were grotty, blah blah blah. It was a downward spiral.'

Martin agrees: 'It's really difficult to find the rent or the mortgage interest if you're an arts charity. You do well just to wash your face on current expenditure.' Lucas Shoemaker, who set up Stroud Common Wealth with Martin, looks back now and says: 'And arts as the first project for a small company like Stroud Common Wealth is digging a huge hole for yourself.'

Stroud Common Wealth were also engaged in other projects which have brought different expertise and prosperity to Stroud. They started a small social enterprise office off the High Street and took on The Exchange building on Brick Row. Max Comfort tells the story: 'The Exchange is financially viable, it's self-sustaining; we've repaid a five-year loan from a charity bank in four years; it's attracted something like £250,000 worth of capital into Stroud through grants; and it's contributed around £25,000 or £30,000 a year to the Stroud economy. We've completely refurbished this small stone building, originally Stroud's first girls' school. It's very energy efficient, in that all the heating is underfloor, run by a ground source heat pump and photovoltaic panels on the roof. The building's fully accessible, which is important in Stroud as most of the buildings aren't because of the steepness and so on. It's now become a sort of Stroud icon, and it's full, with a waiting list. So it's a social enterprise success story.'

Stroud Common Wealth also set up Gloucestershire Land for People and over the past nine years have been working on and developing the old hospital site at Cashes Green. Max Comfort is in charge of the project: 'This was the first ever urban Community Land Trust in the UK. 78 new homes are being built, designed by Kevin McCloud's Haboakus company, and the site, having worked hard to get the whole community involved, will now be run by a local Community Land Trust of local residents.'

However, the charity running Lansdown Hall and Gallery was not able to manage the repairs needed for this listed building and so they approached the Town Council for financial help in 2009. The mayor of Stroud at the time, Andy Read, told the full Council that there was an emergency situation and that The Space was in danger of failing. Councillor Steve Hurrell remembers the meeting. 'We were worried that what was seen as a really good, vital arts community resource might go into the private sector, be sold, and become possibly a place for development for habitation and so on, and we'd lose a vital resource,' he says. They discussed whether the Town Council should step in and find a way to prop it up, but they didn't think it could be propped up in the way it was being managed. The Town Council commissioned a survey of the building and a valuation and found they could get a Public Works Board Loan on relatively favourable terms, so they decided to buy it. 'The main reason for doing it, from the Council's

'At the Seaside' fundraising event

point of view,' says Steve, 'was to make it in a sense our community or village hall – because the Town Council is actually what's called a town parish council, unlike the District Council. It really only represents the people who live within the walls of the town.'

Steve became part of a working group, liaising with an architect and a property surveyor who had previously worked for the Council, and they started to think about what the building needed and the way forward. 'The first thing we needed to make sure of was that the Trust itself was able to keep running. At that time Jeremy Collingwood was recently appointed as the Chair of the Trustees, and we've been in constant dialogue with him ever since.'

The building had suffered through a lack of maintenance, and the Council's first job was analysing, assessing and finding out what needed to be done. They set about doing emergency repairs, which were to the drainage from the roof. The building's stonework was falling to bits in places, but the damage meant that the gutters were all blocked and water was just running down the building. Another immediate problem was that the heating system collapsed and a new gas boiler had to be installed. 'So even though we're a Green Council and we wanted to try to actually address the building with a low carbon footprint,' says Steve, 'we had to immediately put in a new gas boiler, although our objective long term will be to use more efficient energy savings such as air to heat pumps.'

'The first stage was the repairs and the emergencies,' says Steve. 'Phase two was separating the Gallery and the Hall and providing disability access to the Gallery. Phase three will be the strengthening of the floor of the building to make sure that the floor is supported properly. And phase four will be the building of a wholly new entrance into the building from Bank Gardens.' This will provide an 'access for all' from the High Street, all on one level. Upstairs in the Hall there are further plans: to move the bar to the tower, which will have a mezzanine across it (where the stairwell used to be); to install a new toilet block; and to build a new extension. This will be a two- or three-floor extension at the far end of the building which will allow room for greater storage, for a

Green Room for performers, backstage area improvements and extra storage.

At the time of writing, the Council is in the process of looking for funding for these projects. 'As owners of the building, we're responsible for the physical asset,' says Steve, 'so we obviously have to maintain it, and we have got some earmarked funds to add in, because you often need matched funds to show that you're investing before others will invest.'

The maintenance of the building has kept everyone busy, he says, with new fire alarms, lighting, and so on. 'In a way, when it was first set up this was never envisaged. Gloucestershire County Council sold the property to an arts group, but this overall holistic planning about how you maintain it for a future of 100 years or more and keep the building safe was never actually done. That's why it fell into disrepair. So we're making sure that this is the first thing that we do, not the last,' he says.

Jeremy Collingwood, current Chair of the Trustees, became involved in what was still called The Space when he was using the building while organising the 2009 Fringe Festival and Sue Bearder told him a new trustee was needed. He asked to be made Chair and took over from Jo Bousfield. She remembers their first meeting: 'He said, I will put people's backs up – that's what'll happen – people will be offended. And immediately there were things that happened. People were sacked. And I thought, good on you, because he was really clear about it. But the amazing thing about Jeremy is that he's completely hands on, he has his number on the wall and he'll come down here whenever.'

Jeremy soon realised The Space was in a very large financial hole. 'It was ruled by people's hearts, not their heads. They were using grants to pay wages, that kind of thing. No one was sitting there going oh my God... Strictly, we were trading at half past twelve, as it were, because there's no way we could have paid our debts. Meetings went on interminably and nothing was ever agreed. I love the arts but I've got a business background.'
The first thing Jeremy tackled was the question of what function the building could have. Prema and Stroud Valleys Artspace were getting national funding from the Arts Council. The Space's funding was being cancelled because no

one was employed, and the District Council funding was disappearing. 'We were finding it harder and harder to get any grants at all, because we just employed one person at 20 hours a week, and also no one wanted to get involved in something that was falling apart,' he says. 'The drains were blocked and there were power failures, the lights didn't work, there was no hot water in the kitchen.' Jeremy thought the place should be a community venue. 'We had a clear plan that would focus on providing the best quality services we could at the cheapest price, and also that the Board would stop being a discussion about the arts in Stroud and start being about what we were doing and who was doing what. And basically if you couldn't be an active Board member you should leave. Some people stayed; other people just left.'

The new Board changed the name from The Space to Lansdown Hall & Gallery.

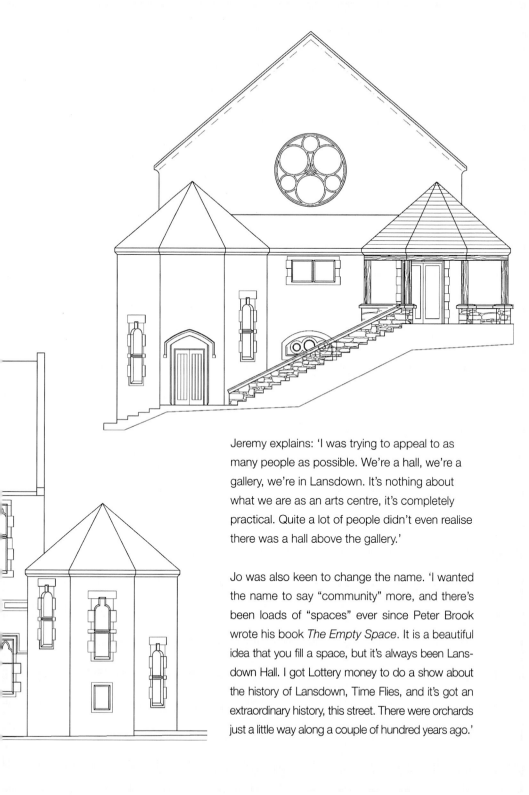

Jeremy explains: 'I was trying to appeal to as many people as possible. We're a hall, we're a gallery, we're in Lansdown. It's nothing about what we are as an arts centre, it's completely practical. Quite a lot of people didn't even realise there was a hall above the gallery.'

Jo was also keen to change the name. 'I wanted the name to say "community" more, and there's been loads of "spaces" ever since Peter Brook wrote his book *The Empty Space*. It is a beautiful idea that you fill a space, but it's always been Lansdown Hall. I got Lottery money to do a show about the history of Lansdown, Time Flies, and it's got an extraordinary history, this street. There were orchards just a little way along a couple of hundred years ago.'

One of the first jobs done right at the beginning of Sue starting was the opening up of the Gallery on the ground floor. It used to be a room that was not much used. Sue and former manager Rick Vick decided to remove the old brown carpet and strip the floor, and recently Stroud Town Council raised the funds to open the pavement entrance door and make the whole gallery fully accessible. 'I'm really pleased with the new entrance,' says Jo. 'That's something I've wanted for years – to use that central door, which is a beautiful old door. And the new sign, which is really beautiful and modern, looks great. Stroud can really cope with galleries. There are so many artists here and there are surprisingly few galleries.'

'And there's such a nice atmosphere in there,' adds Sue. 'People love it, and they feel like it's friendly, anyone can come in. I've got lots of bookings already for next year.'

Jeremy also welcomed the literal and figurative opening of the front door to allow access for all. 'Obviously for the disabled,' he says, 'but for me it was letting people back into the building and welcoming the community.'

Jeremy started recruiting help. 'We wanted volunteers who were skilled and able to do something,' he says. 'And we also reached out to various other local people. For instance, the bar in the Hall had collapsed and was falling to pieces. We spoke to Woodchester Cabinet Makers, and they designed, built and fitted a new bar for materials cost only – £800, fantastic. Customers were getting splinters in their feet from the Hall floor, which hadn't been maintained for many years, and Matt did a fantastic job at an unbelievably cheap price.'

'Expectations were rising all the time, particularly in terms of technology, so we started improving everything in the Hall. The Hall sound system was complete rubbish, so D&B Audio in Nailsworth – they were very, very helpful – came and did a free audio survey of the Hall and they made an audio map of the Hall so we knew where the issues were. They helped us reposition the speakers, because the speakers were in completely the wrong place and had been mounted incorrectly. We have also improved the acoustics – that has really helped all the performances.

'When the Council put the new power supply in they also put in a new power supply behind the stage and, with the help of various skilled local technical people, we moved all the hi-fi equipment ourselves to a new place served by the new power supply. We achieved a massive improvement in the hi-fi, which, had we gone out and paid to get it done, would have cost £10,000 or something. We did it all ourselves. The other thing was that it was very difficult to use, and obviously nowadays people expect technology to be easy to use, so we instigated customer controls, so that anyone can now use the house PA.'

Jeremy is a great believer in technology being a liberator. 'Now you can just light up the window beds, and it's instant atmosphere,' he says. 'You can either have solid colours or change them around. It's new technology, and LEDs are fantastic things. It's like a light switch and, again, customer-controlled so you don't need any technician. I love all that kind of stuff.'

There's a new projector and a new screen. 'We put in a new wi-fi network,' says Jeremy, 'so you can have your laptop, stream, access the web.'

'We're buying second-hand equipment on eBay, which saves us a lot of money,' he continues. 'We just bought a new lighting desk – £3,000 new, £700 on eBay, from some guy whose business has folded – sensible shopping.' Health and Safety's a lot better. The input from local, engineer-trained people reflects the many skills of Stroud. 'It's enabled us to achieve loads.'

Jeremy and the trustees have set out to be broad-cast, not narrow-cast, in order to attract as many different types of people as possible. So the building has held non-denominational funerals, parties, folk bands, rock bands, and there is a regular programme of classes during the day.

Jo Bousfield has used the hall for many things over the years: 'I love that one night you can have a band, one night a show. I've run my youth theatre company, Flies on the Wall, here, and Dramarama as well, and they've been going

Top: The Space quarterly listings brochures
Below: Dramarama children's theatre workshop

for a very long time. I've run creative writing courses, I've had parties here, my daughter had her funeral here. It's a really important building.'

'I think what I'm pleased about is that people now come and have a good experience,' says Jeremy. 'It's brought everything together. We've been able to improve the facilities for a lot of different users – you've got yoga people who want it quiet and warm and zumba people who want it bright and loud, so everything we do has got flexibility in it. We want as much flexibility as possible. We seem to have managed to achieve that, in the sense that the drama groups are happy, the yoga groups are happy, the five rhythms dancers are happy – all the user groups are happy. The three community choirs too – because even though we've deadened it, it still sounds better for choirs than it did before.'

The Board now meets less often and essentially oversees the administration and finance. The volunteers are proactive, and talk to Sue about what's happening and to the hirers about their issues. 'It's great,' says Jeremy, 'we've got younger people, we've got people coming up to retirement – a cross-pollination of younger and older people working together and learning from each other. You can see the sparks coming off. There's a community of people working and a wider community who are using it, and it's not that exclusive thing, which I'm not a big fan of. It's starting to reflect the eclecticism of Stroud. And I'm really pleased about that.

'When I grew up in Stroud there was that cheek-by-jowl thing – the hippies got on with the people who owned the farms, who got on with the people who worked down at Redler's. It was that kind of eclectic mix. There are very few towns I've visited that have that. Stroud's got higgledy-piggledy housing, a non-conformist past, lots of artists. To me that's the charm of Stroud.'

Interviewees: *Sue Bearder, Jo Bousfield, Jeremy Collingwood, Steve Hurrell, Martin Large, Max Comfort*

Top: Punch and Judy audience in the Museum courtyard
Below: Stratford Park Mansion, now Museum in the Park with new gallery wing

8

The New Millennium

The Museum in The Park 2001

'Over the last five years we've really worked hard on advocacy, word of mouth and being involved in projects, so that we now get asked our opinion on things, we get asked to come to a table to discuss Stroud and how we might help to attract people to the area, improve signage, whatever it might be. I think that's an acknowledgement that this project has been successful and that we now have a big role to play in the local community and the area.'

Kevin Ward
Development Manager, The Museum in The Park

STROUD HAS HAD ITS OWN MUSEUM for well over 100 years. A local landowner, William Cowle, left a bequest in his will in 1897 for a museum to be built in the town. Cowle was a grocer and owned the Field Estate, where the hospital is now. Cowle wanted the museum to be located at his observatory, currently the site of the Maternity Hospital, but his trustees on his death decided on the School of Science and Art building in Lansdown. Two rooms there were set aside for the Cowle Museum, as it was then known. There was no curatorial staff until 1930. Then slowly public access began to increase and the museum took on three further rooms, partly for storage and partly to expand the displays.

There was a considerable geology and archaeology collection, which the museum still possesses. Over time, social history was viewed as more important and people started donating things. 'The result of that was that the museum could only display a very small proportion of its collection,' says the current Development Manager for the Museum in the Park, Kevin Ward, who's worked there since 2007, 'much less than we do now.' The collections were distributed in multiple stores off site. 'I think there were about fifteen or so of those!' he adds. Alan Caig, former Head of Leisure at Stroud District Council, remembers that some of the sites were leaking.

Up until the early 1980s the museum was independent, but then it started to struggle financially.The District Council got involved and a partnership was set up whereby the council would provide the funding for the service, i.e. the building and staff, and the Cowle Trust would make the collections available. This arrangement still continues to this day.

'The first phase of the museums development was led by Sue Haywood,' continues Kevin, 'and addressed the collections management side of things, and the off site storage. The second stage was then to seek alternative premises for the museum because really it had outgrown the venue that it was in. It wasn't befitting of a modern museum and wasn't meeting users' needs.'

Among the many possible venues considered, including the Mansion House in Stratford Park where the collection eventually ended up, were the Hill Paul building, Brimscombe Port depot, Stanley Mill and Kimmon's Mill. The Mansion House was eventually chosen, despite its poor state of repair. The Council already owned it and had earmarked funds for improving it. The Grade II listed building had been in private ownership up until 1935, the last owner stipulating that when he died he wanted the mansion and parkland to pass into public ownership. The then Stroud Urban Council purchased the site with the help of a government grant and built the bowling green, the tennis courts and the outdoor lido. The mansion was converted into apartments, and at times was also occupied by a children's nursery and a café. By the late 1980s or early '90s it was dilapidated and empty.

The Heritage Lottery Fund was fairly new in the late '90s. 'There was optimism in the air about the opportunities it offered,' recalls Alan Caig. The project required financial and political support from SDC and Alan remembers that this was not always certain, with power changing hands several times, sometimes resulting in a hung council. Alan also remembers being alarmed to find a statement in some funding documents that the HLF might not be able to pay the £1.8m the museum had been awarded if insufficient lottery money was collected. In fact, the Museum in the Park turned out to be one of the Fund's earliest successful projects.

Kevin Ward puts the successful bid down to the area's heritage. 'Stratford Park is an arboretum, and although there isn't any documentary evidence we believe that the tree specimens were picked at the same time as Westonbirt's. And then you've got the history of Stratford Park estate, of the Mansion House and its adjoining walled garden.'

Lots of individuals and organisations got behind the project, not least the Council, the Friends of the Museum and the Cowle Trust. 'Heritage Lottery eventually committed just over £1.8m to a £2.5m project,' says Kevin. 'The Council put in £486,000. The Cowle Trust committed £33,000 of its funding, Friends £22,000 and the Museum and Galleries Commission £40,000. The South West Museums Council gave a further £9,000, and then there was about £27,500 in kind contributions from members of the public and fundraising activities towards the project.'

What about the people of Stroud and how were they involved? 'To my knowledge there was a development and advisory group and that met on a number of occasions,' says Kevin. And Alan Caig recalls that Sue Hayward brought together research groups to discuss the collections and identify what people wanted from the museum. Proving that the museum was needed and that local people were involved was important to the success of the bid.

Initially there was no plan for an extension, but this was eventually included as part of the bid, since the new building, designed and built by Kier, meant the museum could put on temporary exhibitions and hire out rooms. Also, it sits on the same footprint as previous, long-derelict outbuildings.

However, the move to Stratford Park was not without opposition. Some people

Top: Building the new gallery and foyer wing
Below: The foyer just before opening

objected to the fact that the museum would be too far away from the town centre, and others had definite views about its location. 'There were definitely parts of the community who wanted the Hill Paul building particularly, the argument for it being that it would be big enough to include all the collections,' says Kevin. And matters became complicated when the Friends of the Museum and what became known as the Stroudwater Textile Group split in the early 1990s, the textile group taking with it a lot of industrial and textile-related artefacts. 'But from my understanding I think it came down to what could the Council basically afford, as always,' continues Kevin.

Converting the building into a museum uncovered some of its history and led to the discovery that it used to have three floors. There's also a story about a Mrs Hallowell, who passed away and whose wake was held in one of the rooms; the story is that bells rang from that room but when someone went in it was empty. In fact there are servants' bells in the collection, and the museum is thinking now that it might display these and perhaps tell that little anecdotal story as part of the history of the mansion.

As far as the layout of the museum was concerned, it was decided to have a non-linear thematic display. 'The idea behind that is that it gives you a lot more flexibility,' says Kevin. 'It's then a case of deciding what the themes are and looking at the objects that will support that story. Obviously you've got the big notable ones like the Budding lawnmower, the adjustable spanner, the Pederson bicycle, mammoth tooth and tusks.' The team had to ensure that the themes chosen told the broad history of the area, from the earliest times up to the modern day, with a strong focus on people and people's stories.

'It was also decided very early on that the displays would be object-rich, so there's less text and the objects are not full of labels,' says Kevin. 'This brings challenges because sometimes people want to know what things are, so over a period of time we've have information cards introduced. We now have downstairs a box of information sheets that cover every single display case, with itemised lists of what's in them.'

From the beginning, there's been an emphasis on welcoming families and children. 'I think even in those early days it was clear that a family audience would be our biggest audience and that's grown exponentially since then,' says Kevin. But the museum is trying to cater for other audience groups as well. 'Audience groups can be broad for a museum like this,' Kevin continues, 'but we're introducing things like trails. Trails are a very good way of getting people to interact and look at the collections that are on display in more detail.'

'They say that museum visitor numbers rise in times of recession,' continues Kevin, 'because people want to find their place in the world, and we seem to help to provide a connection with the wider community.' As a result of positioning itself in the community the museum finds that it has been consulted more in matters to do with Stroud's future. 'Over the last five years we've really worked hard on advocacy, word of mouth and being involved in projects, so that we now get asked our opinion on things; we get asked to come to a table to discuss Stroud and how we might help to attract people to the area, improve signage, whatever it might be,' says Kevin. 'I think that's an acknowledgement that this project has been successful and that we now have a big role to play in the local community and the area.'

Many outside organisations bring people with special needs to the museum so that they can engage with what's on display. The museum also participates in something called 'Art on Prescription' – a referral service, run by the College, which uses the venue because of its relaxing parkland setting.

Plans for the future include the development of the Grade II listed adjoining walled garden. When the Museum in the Park project finally happened there was a small lobby area created in the reception area, from where you could go out into the garden. However, the museum's first priorities, as part of a five-year development plan starting in 2007, were getting itself positioned in the community and addressing deficiencies in collections management. 'This was through no fault of my predecessors,' says Kevin. 'It's a huge step from where they were, and so of course there were things that had to take a back step.' The staff completed an audit of all of the collections so that they knew

Top: Select 2013 private view
Below: Stroud College student drawing in Gallery One

where everything was, and could start justifying why they had these objects, as well as going through a rationalisation process and disposing of certain things. 'The last five years I think have been very successful for us,' says Kevin. The museum has started a café for visitors, the volunteer base has increased, and visitor numbers have risen from 29,000 before that five-year plan to 55,000 last year and this year.

In the last year, with the support of the Friends of the Museum, the focus has shifted to the walled garden. 'There'd been lots of ideas for the garden over the years,' says Kevin. 'We've now developed a master plan which features a multi-use learning space which we're calling the Pavilion.' The museum has just been awarded £250,000 by the Gloucestershire Environmental Trust for this, the largest award they have ever given. A dedicated learning space in the garden will cater for a growing demand. Currently the museum welcomes well over 2,000 pupils a year and they have between 55 and 60 school engagements a year.

The other big feature of the development plan is trying to increase access to the stored collections. 'My vision is that I want the local community to know about the collections we have in store, why we have them, the importance of having them and caring for them, but also to hopefully improve access to them,' says Kevin.

Kevin finishes by summing up why he thinks the museum has been such a success: 'Part of it has been getting people involved, so that it's not a one-way street. We try to help other projects, but also we rely heavily on different organisations. For our public programmes, for instance, Stroudwater Textile Trust help us deliver as do the Textile Festival and Stroud Valleys Artspace. We use local actors and there's many other individuals and organisations out there that we work with and who offer their knowledge and expertise to the Museum.

'The success of the project has been down to the people of Stroud, because I believe what we've done is enabled them to buy into us – they own a proportion of the museum, and they can take pride in what we do here and they really love the setting.'

Interviewees: *Kevin Ward, Alan Caig*

Children's archeology workshop in the Museum

9

The New Millennium

Transition Stroud 2006

'Stroud has the mixed blessing of real energy coming into it and alternative ideas about doing things differently, and the problem of everybody doing their own thing. So it's a mixed bag, but it means that Stroud is unique. And it draws to it people who've got that permaculture belief, the feeling that we've got to go green. So we end up with a lot of incomers. If you live in a town or a village and you want to get anything done, ask the new people. All the jobs I've ever done where I've had to get volunteers – I usually train volunteers – I've asked people who've popped in from London, or just moved in from Birmingham. They've come to live here and they want to get active.'

Helen Royall, Transition Stroud coordinator

THE TRANSITION MOVEMENT WAS started by environmental activist Rob Hopkins. A permaculture teacher at Kinsale College of Further Education in Ireland, in 2004 he became aware of the concept of peak oil, setting his students the task of applying permaculture principles to addressing the challenge. The result was the Kinsale Energy Dissent Action Plan (EDAP), which provoked worldwide interest. He then moved to Totnes, taking his ideas with him, and co-founded Transition Totnes and the Transition Network in 2005/6.

Part of Transition's message is putting a positive slant on the future, rather than thinking that nothing can be changed. Rob starts a lot of his talks by describing a scene in Woody Allen's film, *Sleepers*. Woody Allen is in a train and he looks round and all the people are dull, grey and looking bored, and then he looks across at another train and the people there are attractive and colourful and having a party. And then he looks back at his train and it's all very dull again, and he thinks he's on the wrong train. Rob says that when he used to work with environmental concerns it was like being on that grey train, but since he's worked with Transition it's like being on the party train.

His philosophy is based on 'head, heart and hand': think about what you're doing and try to change people's beliefs; talk about your worries and concerns; and go out and get involved.

Transition Stroud coordinator, Helen Royall, explains: 'That's what Transition is about – helping that change, towards something greener and more sustainable. Rob talks in his book about how you used to be able to go to a little village and it was totally sustainable. The food came from that village, the entertainment came from the village, and transport was within the village. And then suddenly with all this cheap petrol, they started getting their food from the other side of the world and they started to be told what to do by someone who didn't actually live in the village, but was managing them from some other country. And suddenly they weren't sustainable. They changed from being a sustainable community to being non-sustainable in a very short time period. And that's what we've got. Here in Stroud, someone in London decided that we needed to close our post office in Ebley. They've never walked down the streets in Ebley, but they told us that was what we had to do. And that, for me, doesn't make sense.'

The Transition Stroud group started meeting in 2006. Initially activists met to discuss oil and climate change. Now there's a third issue – the collapsing economy. At the start, there were already lots of people in Stroud involved in different projects – Stroud Community Agriculture, for example, was already up and running – so it was agreed that everyone would go off and form their own special-interest groups. In 2007 Richard Heinberg, an American educator, gave a talk about peak oil in the Sub Rooms to about 500 people. Transition Stroud wasn't yet constituted, but a year or so later the group decided to form an organisation and Helen Royall became coordinator. They decided to adopt a 'chaordic' method of organisation, which stands for chaos and order combined.

Top: Bike-powered music in Stratford Park
Below: Photovoltaic and vegetable sustainability!

'What it means,' explains Helen, 'is that you have a central idea and you can go off and do anything you like as long as it's part of that central idea. If you wanted, for example, to set up a group of dancers for Transition, you could do that if it was going to help the Transition movement; the movement would support you and you would be covered by their insurance. So the Skills Gain group, for example, sent papers to Transition, saying this is what we want to do and why, and we said this is great, we'll support you, and that's gone from strength to strength. And Edible Open Gardens is running now, and has its own little group that organises it and a life of its own.'

In 2009 Transition Stroud became a company limited by guarantee, a not-for-profit organisation, and in 2011 Seb Buckton was taken on as development officer.

'Having a legal structure enabled Transition Stroud to apply for grants,' says Seb. 'There were two main sources of money, and these led to my role being created. One was the monthly donations that individuals were giving, which got to the level where TS felt they could have someone working there maybe a couple of days a month – actual paid work – to hold some of the core work, do a bit of promotion, that kind of thing. And then they got a grant from the Big Lottery Awards For All – £9,000 – and that then enabled them to expand the role of the development worker to 8 days a month for 12 months.'

At the time of writing, the initial funding is now finished, and Transition Stroud are back to having baseline money which pays for a couple of days of month of Seb and a couple of days a month of Helen.

In those early days, there were not many other Transition Towns in the UK; Transition Stroud was the fourth in the country to be established. There are now 1,000 groups worldwide.

As Helen describes it, Stroud has the mixed blessing of real energy coming into it and alternative ideas about doing things differently, and the problem of everybody doing their own thing. 'So it's a mixed bag, but it means that

Stroud is unique. And it draws to it people who've got that permaculture belief, the feeling that we've got to go green,' she continues. 'So we end up with a lot of incomers. If you live in a town or a village and you want to get anything done, ask the new people. All the jobs I've ever done where I've had to get volunteers – I usually train volunteers – I've asked people who've popped in from London, or just moved in from Birmingham. They've come to live here and they want to get active.'

There are several working groups within Transition Stroud, though these sometimes lack the right people to drive them forward. 'That's probably one of the biggest challenges – that we actually have a fairly small number of people,' says Seb. 'There's a big audience, and lots of people who are interested and want to get involved, but the people who actually drive projects are much smaller in proportion, so if one of them drops out...' Groups currently active include Food (Edible Gardens, Edible Stroud, Stroudco Food Hub), Skills Gain, Transport, Business and the Textile group, which promotes 'make do and mend' skills.

'One of the ways we've tried to organise as a group is thinking about what our aims are,' says Seb. 'We came up with a stage process: initially try to engage with people and raise awareness, then provide people with the opportunities to develop their skills and learn about things, and finally encourage them to actually take action. It's a three-stage thing.' Transition Stroud creates a space for people to network with each other and develop ideas, he explains.

'It's also an educational thing,' adds Helen. 'What we're trying to do is say to people: the oil is running out, the climate's changing, the economy's collapsing, we need to do something. So any project that comes out of it has those three things in mind.'

Some projects started up outside Transition Stroud and have linked into it, like Stroud Community TV, which was something that was developed largely by Philip Booth. It became a working group within Transition Stroud, partly to draw on the structure that the movement has. 'It wasn't like Transition Stroud

Top: Stroud Community TV logo
Below: Open Edible Gardens event

decided we needed to have community TV,' says Seb, 'it was his idea.' The Stroud Pound (developed in 2010) is a good example of something that very much came out of Transition Stroud, but is now something that has its own legal entity. Although it's talked about as being part of Transition Stroud there isn't a legal link between the two.

Transition Stroud's Winterfest event took place in December 2012 in Lansdown Hall. Any related organisations were invited to come along, take a stand for free, and show the public what they were doing. Helen expands: 'I was getting quite dispirited at the end of last year, thinking are we doing anything, is it worth it? I couldn't go to the Winterfest because I'd broken my leg, but I then saw the film that Philip [Booth] made of it and I thought, wow, we're doing loads, it's lovely, look at all these fantastic people. The Winterfest for us was like a celebration of what we'd done through the year.'

Helen and Seb are optimistic about the future of Transition Stroud. 'It's making quite an impact. I think that things are happening,' says Helen.

'We're getting increasing recognition for what we're doing,' continues Seb. 'The District Council have provided us with some funding – certainly last year and probably this year as well – so they recognise that we're delivering something that they can't deliver at the moment for whatever reason. The issues are in the news every day and people are becoming much more aware of it all. The only barrier really is if people haven't heard of Transition.'

Transition Stroud are thinking hard about how to mainstream their movement beyond the environmentally aware. As development officer, it's been part of Seb's role from the beginning. They are hoping for funding from the Town Council to pay for someone to go round Stroud giving talks to schools and community groups.

Although Transition Stroud is more about personal and small group action and less about campaigning, they are linked to various campaigns like Down to Earth, Stroud Valleys Project, Gloucestershire Wildlife Trust,

Stroud Community Agriculture and the Car Club. As a 'bottom up' organisation, Transition Stroud's aim is to do everything locally.

'There are various greenfield developments proposed around Stroud that there are big campaign groups for,' says Seb. 'We don't actively campaign, but we will publicise them. Really what we are is a network and a space for people to be able to talk about things that concern them. And if they're relevant to Transition, we'll promote the discussion with publicity but that's all. As individuals there might well be Transition people who are heavily involved in these things, but not as Transition Stroud, because once you start going down that route you have to do it all the time for everything, otherwise people will say, why aren't you campaigning on this or why aren't you campaigning on that?'

As an environmentally aware town, Stroud has from the beginning embraced and popularised the Transition movement. Seb agrees: 'You're pushing on a lot of open doors and the critical mass is there.'

Interviewees: *Helen Royall, Seb Buckton*

Campaigners save Laurie Lee beauty spot from developers

VALLEY WINS REPRIEVE

■ Joy for
Slad
Valley
dweller
and
famous
author
Laurie
Lee.

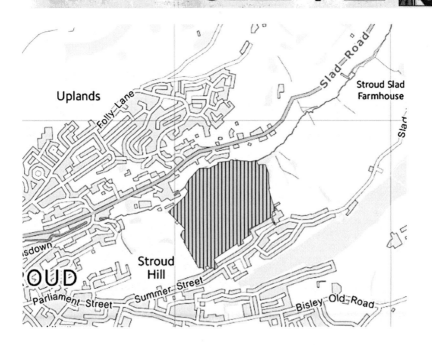

10

The New Millennium

Slad Valley Action Group 1996 & 2013

'We've got a friend in her mid-eighties in Summer Street and she can talk about being involved in campaigns years before we moved to Stroud. So it's interesting how these things just keep repeating – a different generation has to pick up the same sort of issues. Our campaign was successful at the time, but there's been lots of other people doing similar things since – before and since.'

Nick Berry, 1996 activist

THERE HAVE BEEN ANTI-DEVELOPMENT
campaign groups in the Slad Valley since the 1960s and early '70s. Jean and Nick Berry used to live in Summer Street and set up the Slad Valley Action Group in the mid-'90s when Baxter's Field was first under threat. Then it was just the first field that Four Oak developers wanted to build houses on, unlike the 2013 Gladman proposal which encompasses three fields (though this has changed to two on appeal).

Resistance to the Four Oak development seemed to evolve naturally, according to Jean. There'd been some publicity in the local paper and Nick and Jean took leaflets around Summer Street. The resulting group opposing the development was a diverse mix of PR and campaigning professionals, artists, Summer Street residents and others, many of whom didn't even live near the field. Consequently it was more of a Stroud campaign than a very local one. There was no internet then, of course, no Facebook or Twitter, but the campaign still attracted international attention.

'We had people writing to us from Australia and all over the world, amazing at that time when you think, and sending cash in the post as well,' says Nick.

The group decided to name their campaign the Slad Valley Action Group, or SVAG, because they felt strongly that the area was a part of Slad Valley and that the name would resonate with people in Stroud and elsewhere.

'I think if you'd called it Summer Street Action Group, you're on a loser straight away,' says Jean. 'No one cares about Summer Street,' agrees Nick.

Slad Valley has been the subject of other development plans more recently, at Wades Farm (on the north side) and nearer the centre of town at the end of Lansdown. 'I mean it's interesting, because it's just a massive sprawl of houses down there now; they've built on the bottom of the Slad Valley without anybody really realising it,' says Nick. 'And it just looks an absolute eyesore, but it hasn't been handled as Slad Valley, it's just part of the centre of town, brown field redevelopment. Whereas if the Gladman one goes through now, it will clearly be a blot on the landscape from all over the town.'

SVAG held public meetings, and artists became involved. There was an art display with people doing paintings of the Slad Valley and selling them to raise funds. Then there was a big meeting which Laurie Lee came to and spoke at. Nick remembers that there were hundreds of people at the meeting and Laurie, although by then elderly, made a fantastic speech. The campaign carried out traffic surveys and employed someone to do an environmental study – all things to try to support the council and its position.

The development was presented to the council but they rejected it. 'We assumed there'd be an appeal,' says Nick, 'but it never happened, the developers just withdrew. Whether it was because of the weight of public support, I don't know really. Because there weren't that many campaigns in those days, particularly against land developers; now there are so many campaigns it's hard for people to get the profile.'

Nick and Jean felt they learnt some lessons from the campaign. 'You do need diverse people involved, because one of the problems is everybody starts to say well, I'm a vegan and unless you're vegan then I won't, or unless you're vegetarian or whatever it is, and we always try to say, let's focus on the issue here, because when you do get diverse people it actually adds incredible strength,' says Nick. 'At Slad Valley Action Group, we had artists doing paintings, we had singers doing songs, we had people writing letters, we had the bureaucrats like us. Everybody working together is incredibly powerful.'

'And I don't remember us falling out, which I think is quite unusual for a bunch of volunteers,' adds Jean.

Nick and Jean were involved with the campaign for about three years, although of course the campaign wasn't high profile for all that time. When they moved house, they passed on all their paperwork to Eric Jarrett, the chair of SVAG when the current campaign started up. 'We knew it would happen again at some point,' says Nick, 'though we never thought it would actually spill all the way down as they are suggesting now, all through the fields.'

The group's working methods seem to have been part of its success. 'It's about being clear of your facts and when the plan is in process concentrating on the things that could stop that process from going through,' says Nick, 'you know, work out what are the vulnerabilities and target those things, because it's ever so easy to have a good idea and get distracted into doing just the interesting things. I suppose it's about trying to focus on the right things.'

Jean thinks it's also about being businesslike. 'Allocate tasks to people efficiently, make sure they carry those tasks out, because one or two people can't do everything. You need to share the burden, share the load.'

Jean recalls doing stunts as well. 'I remember going to the District Council one morning with a huge easel and a board. We'd taken this board and easel everywhere round town and people signed it and when it was full of hundreds and hundreds of signatures we took it to the Stroud District Council. You have to make it lively and interesting.'

'Engaging with the local press is obviously important, and with the councillors as well,' adds Nick. 'I think we did say to Eric with this 2013 campaign that it's important that you get your local county and district parish councils on board because they're the decision-makers.'

Nick and Jean have not been so involved in the current campaign over Baxter's Fields, though they have helped write letters, shared their resources and views, and gave advice. They were asked if it was OK to use the SVAG name, which they readily agreed to. 'You can't really improve on that name, and it's already in some people's heads, and it's the same fields, it's the same issues, so it made sense to carry on using it,' says Jean.

Other people who were involved at the same time as Nick and Jean have now reached their 70s and didn't feel they had the energy for the current campaign. And now, of course, new technology has changed the way campaigns work. 'I can't believe that we achieved what we did achieve without all the social media,' says Jean.

Nick thinks technology now plays a huge role. 'You'll get older people saying, we're not interested in Twitter or Facebook or whatever, but actually you haven't got a choice, you have to get someone to run those bits for you because that's the way that young people get involved... so that's a really important learning point for groups nowadays, which is to cover all your bases. That's why the diversity thing is so important, because you don't want all old fuddy duddies like us, you want young people. Groups fall out because they think everyone should be ideal replicas of them.'

The SVAG campaign was all about saying no to development, so what about saying yes to something? 'Saying no can be quite energy sapping and it appears you're against change,' says Jean, 'but once they see the fields I think people understand what we're talking about. What attracted us to Summer Street were the fields, the fact that you could be outside and you could almost

Cartoon by Katy Cambridge for the campaign against development in Baxter's Fields, 2013

Let's keep it
The Slad Valley

'Slad Valley – Stroud End' by Noela Bewry, photographed by Tony Moth

not
The Sad Valley!

Join Slad Valley Action Group's
fight to protect our fields.
For further information contact
Stroud 754522 or 764231

Early campaign poster from SVAG 1996 featuring local artist Noella Bewry's painting

be in rural France. The expression 'green lung' is very apt for that area – you can walk into town but you've still got those fields alongside the houses.'

'Our counter argument at that time was purely about alternative, more appropriate sites,' continues Nick. 'There was talk about trying to buy the fields after that and turning it into like a community orchard of something, but of course the moment the pressure of the campaign diminishes everybody just falls away and you just wait for the next thing to happen again really.

'We've got a friend in her mid-eighties in Summer Street and she can talk about being involved in campaigns years before we moved to Stroud,' he continues, 'so it's interesting how these things just keep repeating – a different generation has to pick up the same sort of issues. Our campaign was successful at the time, but there's been lots of other people doing similar things since – before and since.'

Moving on to 2013, and the same issue is indeed being repeated. The Slad Valley is again under threat of a housing development on Baxter's Fields, this time proposed by developers Gladman. The next interview, with Shawn Jarrett, was recorded in March 2013.

Shawn lives in Summer Street very close to the proposed development and only recently moved to Stroud. She explains why she got involved in SVAG: 'I have been very involved and run campaigns in the past that were protesting against what people felt were inappropriate development, especially in Norfolk where I lived before. I thought that I was moving somewhere where the landscape was protected because it's quite a special landscape across the street. When I found it wasn't and that it was under threat, I was so impressed with the work the group was doing that, even though I'd sworn never to get involved in anything like that again, I have – I couldn't not be involved really.'

Shawn heard rumours about the development and contacted Eric Jarrett (no relation) about it. She didn't know about the earlier campaigns in the area, though she knew a certain amount about Wades Farm. Housing legislation has changed since then, but she still felt her experience had some relevance and that she could contribute as an activist.

'I'm good at finding angles on things, checking facts and talking to people and getting them to tell me things,' she says. She does whatever SVAG ask her to do. 'I've designed some posters for the big planning board meeting at Ebley Mill, and I've written a song. I've a history of playing in Antony Blue Street Band and things like that, so I've often approached political things through the arts because I find that you can disarm people and somehow, if you sing something to them, they listen.'

Shawn has done a lot of leafleting in town with positive results, has encouraged people to sign letters at Black Books Café, and gives support to busy people in SVAG by phoning people and checking facts. 'I'm happy to be in a support role for this one, because I'm new to the area and because the committee itself had already made such a good head start,' she says.

There are lots of challenges in the campaign and problems to overcome. 'One thing is the ambiguous nature of the new legislation which no one really understands,' says Shawn. 'Another thing is the fact there's a campaign at Rodborough Fields and there's vey much a 'let's sit back and see what happens' attitude, because if that site goes, we're more likely to be saved.' Shawn explains that there had been an idea for the two campaigns to work together to form a Stroud-wide campaign but it sadly didn't come off.

The problems the campaign faces are essentially the relationships both with the planning system and the planning authority, and with the developers. Shawn explains what's currently happening in planning. 'The end of this month [March] is when the District's current Local Plan runs out, so from that point on Stroud is easy pickings… But I do know that, for example, the fields across the street do not form part of the District Council's core building strategy.'

One unintended result of the exhibition that Gladman put on to explain the development was the way it got people together. 'The exhibition was fairly useless as a piece of information, but in terms of getting people talking to each other and discussing their concerns it was great and a lot of energy came out of that,' says Shawn. Early on in the campaign, lots of people offered to help but some of that information got lost, Shawn thinks, just because there was so much to do. 'The group has focused very much on the legislation because I think the consensus is that unless we're very unlucky Stroud District Council will turn this down,' she continues, 'but then it will go straight to appeal, and everyone is already thinking about that and focusing on it because that's where the really detailed, accurate kind of work has to happen.'

She believes that people in Stroud, being used to campaigns, are generally sympathetic and ready to listen, and there has been a very healthy response. When she spoke to the council recently to complain about her letter not appearing on the website, they said they'd been totally inundated and were way behind.

But not everyone is strongly against the development. Shawn has found people's reactions to the development interesting. 'I think there is a general recognition that housing is needed, so some people will say well we need houses therefore I'm not interested because they need to be built somewhere and that's as good as anywhere else. Other people say, oh it's a done deal, there's no point in protesting, and other people say, oh I didn't know that was happening, and then there are the people who do know and are already doing their own research. But it's generally been a very positive response.'

Of the people who are writing to the council, there are only three letters in favour so far, and all of them are from the family who own the land. Those against include quite a few people who were involved in the Wades Farm campaign. And there have been a lot of letters from the young people of Stroud, from ages seven to eighteen.

Leafleting has uncovered some people who are very keen on direct action, says Shawn, including sitting down in front of bulldozers and not necessarily following the purely legislative route. Although it's something she feels SVAG would be uncomfortable with, she likes the idea of different approaches. 'That's a feature of most campaigns that attract wide support. People have different skills, different aptitudes and so they will approach things in completely different ways.'

She feels very positive about the campaign so far. 'I'm hugely impressed with the amount of work people have put in and their focus on the kind of detail which is going to matter later on, I think. I think they are being incredibly professional about it and I'm in awe of that. I think in terms of rallying, engaging other people to feed information in, that's got better and better. It's improved just over the last month, which I think is excellent, and there seems to be a storm of letters all coming in at the last minute as well, so that's good.'

Some of the events the campaign have put on, however, haven't always been very well publicised. 'In my experience you can set up the most wonderful event, but if you don't put as much energy into the publicity you've kind of wasted your time, so there've been several events about letter-writing and maybe we've had ten letters come out of them, if that,' she says. The information is out there, but what's difficult is motivating people to look for it.

SVAG also tried to link their campaign with national campaigns. 'There was disagreement within the committee about whether that was the route to go or whether analysing and rebutting the NPPF [National Planning Policy Framework] was what they should be concentrating on,' says Shawn. 'The NPPF has been seen as a charter for developers and builders. In fact the *Telegraph*, which is probably not a paper I would normally buy, has been running the most wonderful series of articles about the effects that the new planning legislation is going to have and I was hoping that we could link up with that. I did write to the *Telegraph* but I didn't get anything back.'

Gladman claim that the District Council put them onto the Baxter's Field site. 'They said they were looking at four sites,' says Shawn, 'and this was the one that was recommended. Now if that's true it could have been because they thought this

Giant letter presses home valley protest

Jeanne Berry presents council official Ian Gobey with the letter. Inset Laurie Lee

By Beverley Hawes

Author backs fight to save beauty spot

A HUGE protest letter signed by almost 1,000 people

Four Oaks plan to build 90 red-brick houses in Slad Valley fields off Summer Street. This is no joke.

Save the Slad Valley!

Slad valley group

Top: Thousands of signatures go to Ebley Mill, 1996 (Western Daily News)
Below: Baxter's Fields campaign leaflet, 1996

was the one they could defend, but equally...' She laughs. 'But if you look at the current pattern of development then you can see there's a nice round shape they could make if they fill in these fields up to the boundary of the AONB.'

As far as the future goes, Shawn feels that it's time to put pressure on the council to have a new plan in place. 'I was speaking to one of the councillors who said, you know if this is defeated they will come back, and I know that. And we've got down five applications behind where I live and so you have to be prepared for that, it doesn't really end just because the district council says no, if they say no. So you have to keep lobbying and you have to try and widen the issues. What the developers try to do is to treat everything separately and it's our job to string all the issues together.'

The Gladman outline planning proposal to build up to 140 residential units was thrown out unanimously by the District Council planning committee, after 1,000 letters of objection were received. As of the end of September 2013, an appeal against Stroud District Council's decision has been put on hold. The planning inspector has opted to suspend the start of the inquiry in the light of complaints from the authority and campaigners about changes made by the developer to the plans. The delayed enquiry will allow residents to be properly consulted about the new plans, in which the number of homes has been reduced to 112, covering two out of the three original fields.

And so the planning debate on housing and green field sites go on, in Rodborough Fields, in Leonard Stanley, in Kings Stanley, in Cam, against supermarkets in Stroud and Stonehouse. Every one of these planning requests has elicited a local residents opposition group. Stroud District Council are between local plans (although at the time of going to press a new draft Local Plan is out for consultation), planning law has changed and the opportunity for development and dissent against development is ripe.

Interviewees: *Nick Berry, Jean Berry, Shawn Jarrett*

Epilogue

THE TEN PROJECTS OUTLINED IN THIS book are also part of the economic success of Stroud. Renovation, regeneration and a business and cultural resurgence have brought in millions of pounds of investment. Other projects not written about here – Stroud Valleys Artspace, the Stroud International Textile Festival, the Cotswold Canal Trust, Woodchester Mansion, Dr Fosters Travelling Theatre, the Credit Union, Stroud Community Supported Agriculture, Community Land Trusts – all invest or have invested economically into the community. They use local resources and local people to work with them, and bring more millions into the town alongside the hundreds of businesses and manufacturing companies in the Valleys.

Forty years ago a local councillor described Stroud as 'one of the ugliest blots on one of the loveliest landscapes in England'. Local residents and people moving into this landscape and townscape saw the potential and have made an extraordinary change.

There is still much to do to alleviate poverty, to make a community truly inclusive, to keep employment highly skilled and to continue to campaign for the built and natural environment that we love so much. The automatic link to community consultation is still not fully unlocked but there is a new generation of campaigners, economic activists and idealists to move forward. If they remember the campaigns mentioned in this book and build on them, we can look forward to a strong future in the town of Stroud.

Camilla Hale, Stroud Preservation Trust

Appendix

1

Biographies

This appendix is to thank the 32 contributors to 'Stroud a Town Changed by Community Action' and to put a face and story to the names of those who have made such a difference to Stroud.

Keith Morgan
Chapter 1, The Old Convent, Stroud

After training as an architect and working in London, Keith came to Stroud in 1976 with his family to develop the Old Convent as a working community. He has lived and worked at the Old Convent ever since as well as being involved in many other architectural projects.

Tom Bermingham
Chapter 2, Shire Training Workshops

Tom brought his family to Stroud for education at the Waldorf School in Brookthorpe after training at Emerson College. After Shire Training Workshops he did a theology degree and has always been involved in buildings work and in community development. He still lives in the Stroud valleys.

Patrick Mansfield
Chapter 2, Shire Training Workshops

After a sociology degree and travelling Patrick came to Paradise House in the mid-'70s and was one of the early team on Shire Training Workshops. He has worked with hundreds of young people in community projects and through Stroud College ever since.

George Perry
Chapter 2, Shire Training Workshops
George came to Stroud in 1976 to set up a shop in Gloucester Street. A trained teacher, he was involved for many years with Shire Training Workshops as part of the initial team and later as trustee. He is an organisational development consultant and heads education development at Emerson College.

Lucas Shoemaker
Chapter 2, Shire Training Workshops
After studying urban planning in his native Holland, Lucas studied at Emerson College in Sussex and farmed and became a plumber all before joining Shire Training Workshops at the end of the '70s. He has been involved in community projects and consultation work ever since and still lives in Stroud.

Claire Mould
Chapter 2, Shire Training Workshops
Claire started as a teacher, completed her PhD in neurology, became a senior research fellow. In 2000 she established her own training and development company working with marginalised community groups to make higher education opportunities accessible. In 2010 Claire became OPENhouse's CEO.

Anne Mackintosh
Chapter 3, Stroud Preservation Trust
Having moved to Stroud in 1972 and horrified to discover plans to demolish historic listed buildings both for a new ring road and in the lower High Street, Anne became a founder trustee of the Stroud Preservation Trust and continues as an active defender of the historic fabric of Stroud.

Clare Mahdiyone
Chapter 4, Stroud Valleys Project

Clare came to Gloucestershire when she was 19. In 1993 she moved to Stroud with her young son, worked with Global Organic Markets and then at The Exchange as a social enterprise advisor. A founder of Stroud FM, she has been CEO for five years with Stroud Valleys Project.

Stella Parkes
Chapter 4, Stroud Valleys Project
Chapter 5, Community Planning Conference

Born and brought up in Stroud, Stella returned as a single mum in the 80s. She has been a local journalist, publicity consultant and manager of the British Heart Foundation shop. Her campaigning has included the SVAG, the CPC, Stroud Valleys Project (20 years) and Stroud Against Supermarket Saturation.

Gerry Robbins
Chapter 4, Stroud Valleys Project

Originally from South Wales, Gerry is a chartered accountant who has worked in Brazil and Kenya amongst other countries. He has had links with Stroud for 30 years, living here for 20. He was a conservation volunteer with Gloucestershire Wildlife Trust and is now Chair of Stroud Valleys Project.

Geoff Beckerleg
Chapter 4, Stroud Valleys Project

An architect with community regeneration projects in London, Geoff moved to Stroud in 1995. He liked the town – 'not posh but with beautiful countryside'. While running an active architects practice he has been trustee with SPT, involved in the Community Planning Conference and is a trustee of Stroud Valleys Project.

Caroline Aistrop

Chapter 4, Stroud Valleys Project

After deciding at 13 that wildlife conservation was her calling, Caroline qualified as a zoologist and worked for The Wildfowl & Wetlands Trust, BTCV, the BBC's Natural History Unit, the RSPB, and for 13 years with Stroud Valleys Project. She now runs her own eco-marketing and PR company, Green Spark.

Chris Smith

Chapter 4, Stroud Valleys Project

In 1989, Chris, an experienced and well known conservation professional, became Stroud Valleys Project's first officer. After six formative years he moved to English Heritage and is now Director of Heritage Protection and Planning. Such is the quality of life in the Stroud valleys that he still lives here.

Mike Goodenough

Chapter 4, Stroud Valleys Project

Chapter 5, Community Planning Conference

'There have been few better places to observe the changes in a town than through the window of the secondhand bookshop I've run for more than thirty years.'

Kaye Welfare

Chapter 4, Stroud Valleys Project

Brought up on a Welsh farm, Kaye's interest has been local community and the environment. She studied Geology, had sales and marketing jobs and in 1993 settled in Rodborough with her family. Since 1997 she has been SDC's energy efficiency officer and Assistant Chief Executive at Severn Wye Energy Agency.

Bill Hicks

Chapter 5, Community Planning Conference

Born Bath 1946 of Cornish parents. Art student, taught in secondary schools England and Zambia. Arrived Stroud thirty years ago. Following redundancy from Stroud College, set-up graphics business for ten years. Been district councillor, currently chairperson of Stroud's talking newspaper. Likes include films, photography, writing, beer, DIY, chums, singing and Stroud.

Alan Mossman

Chapter 5, Community Planning Conference

Now a lean construction consultant and author working around the world with designers, constructors and others involved in creating and maintaining the built environment. In 1995, when initiating the CPC, he was interim manager at Stroud Valleys Project and a socio-technical systems consultant. He trained in architecture and organisation development.

Clare Honeyfield

Chapter 6, Stroud Farmers Market

Clare spent her youth in Churchdown and was an active scouts member. She has always been involved in events, organising and started the Made in Stroud crafts fairs. She set up the Stroud Farmers Market and put Stroud on the map. She now runs the Made in Stroud shop.

Kardien Gerbrands

Chapter 6, Stroud Farmers Market

Born in Zambia, Gerb came to Stroud aged 8, and later discovered Glastonbury and the many influences at Starters Café. He has made tongue drums, travelled through Europe, been a psychotherapist and his last 15 years have been deeply involved in running Farmers Markets and the 'Made In' shops.

Sue Bearder

Chapter 7, Lansdown Hall & Gallery (The Space)

In 1985 Sue came to Stroud for a clog dancing performance and stayed. She founded Roughshod, an internationally successful Appalachian clog dance group, and co-ran the Fringe Festival at the end of the '90s. Since 2004 she has been the Lansdown Hall and Gallery administrator.

Jo Bousfield

Chapter 7, Lansdown Hall & Gallery (The Space)

Jo arrived in Stroud in 1979 as a founder member of Dr Fosters Travelling Theatre. She has written, performed in and directed hundreds of shows including the Stroud Community Play (1991) She has run Flies on the Wall Youth Theatre for 20 years. Jo is the community theatre matriarch in Gloucestershire.

Jeremy Collingwood

Chapter 7, Lansdown Hall & Gallery (The Space)

The Stroud-raised Chair of Lansdown Hall & Gallery and the Stroud Fringe Festival returned to the town a few years ago. A reggae & sound system culture expert who has documented the artistic output of Bob Marley and Lee Perry in particular, he runs various vintage sound systems.

Max Comfort

Chapter 7, Lansdown Hall & Gallery (The Space)

Max's work in Stroud includes being a social entrepreneur, community thought-leader and change agent, liking nothing better than the challenge: 'It can't be done!' He is actively involved in affordable housing (Cashes Green Community Land Trust) and affordable work space (The Exchange).

Steve Hurrell

Chapter 7, Lansdown Hall & Gallery (The Space)

After a 'misspent' 20s playing Frisbee, Steve got involved in film production, the environment and photography in the '80s. He first came to Stroud in 1975 as a painter and decorator and came to live permanently in 2003. He is a trustee of SPT and a Stroud Town Councillor.

Martin Large

Chapter 7, Lansdown Hall & Gallery (The Space)

Coming from a family of Yorkshire Dales hill farmers, Martin moved to Stroud in 1981 when lecturing at Gloscat. His family were printers since Caxton's time and he set up Hawthorn Press to provide books for lecturers. He has been at the forefront of the Community Land Trust movement.

Alan Caig

Chapter 8, The Museum in the Park

Alan was Stroud DC's Leisure and Tourism Manager (1989-2000), and oversaw the relocation of the Cowle Museum to the Museum in the Park, except the final few months. He is very proud indeed of what was achieved, and particularly pleased to feature in Nick Cudworth's big picture!

Kevin Ward

Chapter 8, The Museum in the Park

At school in Eastbourne and university in Bournemouth, Kevin's interest in history got him a job at the Eastbourne Military Museum. He became Head of Collections in 2007 at the RAF Museum. He came to Stroud's Museum in the Park as Director attracted by a community museum with potential.

Seb Buckton

Chapter 9, Transition Stroud

Originally a Londoner, Seb travelled, lived in Bristol and worked at Slimbridge as an ecologist. His partner lived in Stroud so he moved here in 2004. A permaculture course gave him confidence to change career and on the last day of the course he got his job with Transition Stroud.

Helen Royall

Chapter 9, Transition Stroud

Arrived in Stroud in 1990 from teaching in Bristol. Her mother is from Stroud and Helen has home educated her daughter here. Always involved in the community, she joined Transition Stroud in 2008.

Jean Berry, Nick Berry

Chapter 10, Slad Valley Action Group

Lived in Cheshire till 1988 and came to Stroud because of jobs in Swindon and Tewkesbury. They bought their house on Summer Street because of views and soon were involved in the threat of development by Four Oaks. Now retired, they are leading the anti-badger cull in Gloucestershire and have set up Gloucestershire Against Badger Shooting.

Shawn Jarrett

Chapter 10, Slad Valley Action Group

Born in New York State and an anthropology student at Cambridge, Shawn became interested in drama and moved to Bristol. Hers was political and educational theatre working with short life housing projects, co-ops, and fighting developments. She had friends in Stroud and came here recently, now retired but still campaigning.

Appendix

2

Stroud Projects Timeline

The following list of community-based organisations and campaigns over the past six decades is bound to have omissions. Apologies to any group or action missed out. The responsibility lies wholly with the authors.

Many of these projects deserve a whole book to themselves and the authors hope that these small acknowledgements of enormous community effort and success will inspire others to write in even more detail the extraordinary story of Stroud's activism over the past 35 years.

To keep this list live and updated please contact:
www.facebook.com/Stroudcommunityaction
and add your comments.

1937

Stroud Arts Festival

Started and financed by the Biggs, the Festival has run continuously except during the war years. Originally a grander, once yearly, festival it now works to bring different cultural events into Stroud and to support smaller events by other groups through the year.

Margaret & Netlam Bigg

1948

Hawkwood College

Founded with an anthroposophical (Steiner) ethos, Hawkwood provides a welcoming context for short courses on the theme of creative exploration, including personal and spiritual development, arts & crafts, music, health & well-being as well as nature and sustainability.

1965

Civic Society

Active for the past 50 years the Civic Society champions good planning, the architectural structure of Stroud, best practice and dynamic debate on the future of the town. It runs a series of talks and visits and challenges planning.

Marie McLoughlin, Mrs Lincoln, Ist Chairman: Arthur Brimsford

1972

Cotswold Canal Trust

After years of basic maintenance, negotiating land and access and feasibility studies, Lottery funding for the restoration of 6km of the canal from the Ocean at Stonehouse to Brimscombe Port was finally clinched in 2006/7. CCT has over 7,000 members, the largest canal society in England.

Ken Burgin, Chief Executive and a member since 1975, Bruce Hall (ex Chair) an early member

1976

The Old Convent

Bought by entrepreneurs Keith Morgan and Peter Waller, this convent built in the 1860s was a huge challenge to restore. It has been the centre of café, theatre and complimentary medicine life in Stroud ever since as well as offering offices for a wide variety of organisations.

Keith Morgan, Bea Morgan, Peter Waller

1976

SCAR (Society Against the Ring Road)

After protests and campaigns the public enquiry cancelled the proposed Ring Road for the town. Several listed buildings would have been demolished and the fly over (near the Old Police Station) would have been 200 yards long and 20 feet at its highest point.

Key activists: Mary Fermor, Clare Toy

1977

Shire Training Workshops

Shire Training Workshops began in the Starters Café in the High Street and then took on the listed British School as a building training project ground for young people using Manpower Services funding. The organisation is now called **OPENhouse**, a community of housing for young people, with workshops and offices.

Tom Bermingham, George Perry, Patrick Mansfield

1978

Stroud Workhouse Preservation Trust

The workhouse was to be demolished. A local trust could not raise funds to buy the building but did make the case for its preservation. It was bought by a property dealer and converted into many flats.

Mike Goodenough

1978

Stroud Women's Refuge

Offering help, advice and support to families affected by domestic abuse. This is a confidential service, run by women, for women and their children.

1980

Stroud High Street Action Group

57 – 62 High Street were to be knocked down. After injunctions from SDC, sitting on the roof, processions, protests and petitions the High Court directed that a local council had to reconsider buildings condemned under the Public Health Act order and repair and renovate where listed.
Key activists: Steve Tomlin, Mike Goodenough, Julian Usborne

1982

Stroud Preservation Trust

Cornhill as a relief road was proposed in 1980. Eventually the other buildings running up into Nelson Street were demolished to make way for Cornhill and the County Council sold the Medieval Hall (then almost in ruins) to the newly formed Stroud Preservation Trust for £1 (1982).
Patron: David Verey. Trustees: Nigel Paterson, Julian Usborne, Anne Mackintosh, Ian Mackintosh, John Thomas, Robin Wichard. Architect: Richard Feilden, Feilden Clegg Design Partnership

1982

Ebley Village By-Pass Action Group

Started by a group of local people to address the increase in traffic through Ebley since the M5 was opened in 1971, the Ebley by pass was finally built in 1994 and was the most environmentally consulted road in Gloucestershire with badger tunnels, local apple trees and native species.

1985

The Meningitis Trust

Stroud's significantly higher cluster of meningitis and her own child being affected stirred Jane Wells into action to set up the Meningitis Trust. It has developed two vaccines, set up help lines to support individuals and sent out thousands of packs of information to all UK doctors and health authorities.
Jane Wells

1983 to 1985

Cycle Paths to Stonehouse and Nailsworth

Manpower Services Commission funding led by Mr Fisher opened up the old railway for walkers and cyclists and for arts projects. Leaflet and interpretation boards were researched and designed by MSC-employed Sarah Parker, Kay Wedgebury, Ian Stuart-Martin and Colin Menendez.

1986

Urbed Report

Funded by Stroud District Council and researched by the Cycle Paths workers, this seminal report high-lighted the value of the 90 or so mills in the valleys to a future for the district.

1986

Green Party politics start in Stroud

John Marjoram is elected for the Green Party and has been a Town and District Councillor ever since.

1986

Ebley Mill purchased by Stroud District Council

This magnificent Mill was bought and fully renovated by Stroud District Council and opened in 1990. Other SDC-owned buildings became available for local communities – the Old Town Hall in Stroud and Kingshill in Cam. The John Street offices were knocked down to make way for the Cornhill shopping development.

1987

The High Street and Kendrick Street are pedestrianised

Cornhill has been built and the 'Berlin Wall' at the top of the High Street holds up the new road. Without these there would not have been pedestrianisation of the High Street and Kendrick Street.

1987

Stroud By Pass

Gloucestershire County Council builds Dr Newton's Way (and does not reinstate the canal).

1987

Stroud History Society

Started with support of the library and has researched many aspects of Stroud's history. An early society in the area – now most large villages have one.

1987

Stroud Valleys Project

Set up to focus on the valleys' built environment and natural and inspired by the Urbed report. The original board was an amalgamation of interested parties including the Chamber of Trade, Gloucester-shire Wildlife Trust, Stroud Preservation Trust, Stroud Civic Society, Gloucestershire Society for Industrial Archeology, Cotswold Canal Trust.

First officer Chris Smith. Management Committee included Anne Mackintosh and Mike Goodenough

1988

Gloucestershire Buildings Recording Group

This was the initiative of Sheila Ely from the National Monument Record at Swindon. Nigel Paterson was one of the initial committee members and became chair in its second year.

Sheila Fry, Nigel Paterson

1988

Woodchester Mansion

Bought by Stroud District Council recognising a unique Victorian gothic treasure. SDC then leased the building in 1989 to the newly formed Woodchester Mansion Trust for 99 years.

1989

Save the Trees

42 mature trees edging Stratford Park were to be felled so that Stratford Road could be widened for access to the new Tesco's site. A seven-month campaign including living in the trees fought traffic calming versus straight, 'safe' roads. The 1990 public enquiry rules for traffic calming.

Ron Birch, who went on to ensure Tree Preservation Orders were in place, Jack Everett, Veronica Woods

1989

The George Hotel, Nailsworth

Saved from demolition in Nailsworth by people sitting on the roof and campaigning. Redeveloped as a mixed use building right in the central cross roads of the town with all its Georgian features saved.

1989/92

Anti poll tax campaign

Stroud joined in with the national anti poll tax campaigns and involved many hundreds of people. The poll tax was cancelled by central government after three years of national battles.

Manny Thain, Debbie Clarke, Chris Moore

1990

LETS and the Stroud Pound

The second Local Exchange Trading system in the UK (after Totnes), the Stroud Pound really took off for some years in the '90s but then lost momentum. A new Stroud pound system was launched again in 2010.

Maggie Mills, Sandra Bruce, Eric von Nida, John Rhodes

1991

Dr Fosters Stroud Community Play

Dr Fosters was part of the Stroud scene since 1979 and created plays for village halls, schools, parks and playing fields. In 1991 over 100 people were involved in the Stroud Community Play and 4000 people came to the show. The play spawned the Community Choir and Community Band.

Jo Bousfield, Joe Hall, Greg Banks, Helen Chadwick, Nigel Stephenson, Kate Loveday

1994

The Old Town Hall

Renovated once the Council moved out and became the volunteer centre and a public space. 400-year celebrations were held through the summer.

1995/6

Community Planning Project (CPC)

Two years of community planning fell flat at the end with the final report focusing so much on culture but gradually many of the final recommendations have been acted on – the request for a town cinema, re-surfacing the Shambles, installing a town manager for some years, etc.

1995

Stroud Valleys Cycle Campaign

The Stroud Valleys Cycle Campaign was set up in the mid-'90s by Jeremy Harris, and then taken on by Sheila Booth. SVCC campaigns for safer roads, better cycling facilities and lower urban speed limits. They have produced a cyclists' map of the Stroud District, and also a Cycling Strategy that is now a council policy document.

Jeremy Harris, Sheila Booth

1995

Stroud Valleys Artspace

At a CPC meeting Jo Leahy and Neil Walker raised the idea of artists' studios. By 1997 they took on a John Street warehouse; they commissioned the market railings, ran the Open Studio and SITE programmes and raised Arts Council funding to renovate the warehouse and take a five-year lease on the Goods Shed.

Jo Leahy, Neil Walker

1996

Slad Valley Action Group

Public enquiry won against the proposal of 90 red brick houses being built in Slad Valley fields off Summer Street. Continued campaigns up to the current day have included Save Rodborough Fields and Wades Farm and are now fighting against development in three Baxters fields.

1996

CPC Shop windows

Empty shop windows negotiated for and used by small community groups displays. Still in action despite there being fewer shops available (32 in 1996).

Anne Mackintosh

1997

Fringe Festival re-invigorated

This really took off from 1997 and musicians and theatre groups from all over the country came to animate the streets of Stroud for the first weekend in September. Now a regular feature on the calendar alongside walking, eating and environmental festivals, September is a month celebrating community action.

Prime movers: Terry Trimmer, John Shepherd, Sue Bearder, Sue Torres

1997

Stroud Valleys Credit Union

This is a local profit-sharing, democratically run financial co-operative offering convenient savings and low interest loans to its members. The members own and manage it themselves. It encourages regular saving, provides loans to members at low rates of interest and helps members manage their financial affairs (if required).

1999

Stroud Farmers' Market

Clare and Kardien Gerbrands, with support at first from Stroud Valleys Project and a grant from SDC, opened this now famous and award-winning Farmers' Market on 4 July 1999. The Made in Stroud shop, in a newly renovated shop space on Kendrick Street, was opened on 1 December 2000.

1999

Lansdown Hall and Gallery

Bought by Stroud Commonwealth from Stroud District Council to keep a community arts space in town. In 2010 Stroud Town Council bought it, again to secure an iconic hall and gallery for the community and to initiate essential repairs and alteration works to bring it into the 21st century.

Stroud Commonwealth, Martin Large

1999 onwards

Stroud Commonwealth

Very varied programme of work including Land for People; The Space; the Cashes Green Hospital development site; and The Exchange on Brick Row for supporting start-up businesses.

1999

Stroudwater Textile Trust

Set up by the textile sub committee of Friends of Stroud Museum to give a greater focus on the Mills and their history. They own a collection of weaving equipment from the valleys, run open days at three mills, collect archive film and photographs and create exhibitions.

2000/2001

Hill Paul Regeneration Group

Hill Paul, an architect-designed late Victorian clothing factory, was threatened with demolition. People sat on the roof, invested their personal money and petitioned against demolition. It was saved and turned into flats with two additional floors. Flats sell well and quickly – and the clock works!

2001

Marah Trust

Founded by six concerned members of Stroud's John Street Baptist Church, Marah's aim is to help the growing numbers of Stroud's men and women who are marginalised by society. Now with over 100 clients and 40 volunteers, Marah is proud that Stroud's Churches work together on this project.

2001

Stroud Museum in the Park

Opened its doors in the former mill owners mansion at Stratford Park after years of dedication and fundraising from Stroud District Council officers. Its popularity rises year on year as people appreciate its local history, its cultural offer to Stroud and the beautiful arboretum setting of Stratford Park.

2001

Stroud Textile Festival (now SIT)

Stroudwater Textile Trust supported the first Textile Festival in 2001 which was run every two years – 2001, 2003, 2005. By 2005 Lizzi Walton was developing the Textile Festival on a more national and international scale. The festival became yearly and an independent organisation, Stroud International Textile Festival, by 2005.

Jane Ford , Lizzi Walton

2002

Stroud Community Supported Agriculture

Formalised from initial meetings the project started in a walled garden providing vegetables. It later expanded to 23 acres at Hawkwood and a further 24 acres in Brookthorpe as an organic self-sustaining vegetable and animal farm. 200 families subscribe and receive weekly veg boxes and regular meat options.

2002 onwards

Stroud's Co Housing

The first Co Housing build in Britain now inspiring many more across the country as people move to the life style that they want in supportive communities.

2002

Story boards around Stroud

Boards all round Stroud tell the histories of the town. Since then Ian Mackintosh has developed maps and walks to go along with this local knowledge.

Ian Mackintosh

2002

Stroud Community Land Trust

Under the aegis of Stroud Valleys Project a charity was set up to take on small bits of land that were abandoned or no longer of use to their communities. To date the trust now hold 24 pieces of land in the parish.

Andy Read, Caroline Aistrop

2003

Stroud Community Car Club

Set up independently and now running out of the Stroud Valleys Project offices and supported by a national organisation, there are three cars available for hire in Stroud so as to reduce second car ownership.

2004

Lansdown Residents Association

An informal group bringing together neighbours. Right from the start the big campaign was the one way system and by 2010 they had got what they wanted. Flies on the Wall youth theatre created 'Time Flies' in 2006, a play and booklet celebrating the history of Lansdown.

2006

Saving Stroud Maternity Hospital

A major campaign to save the maternity hospital for Stroud was launched and won with petitions and marches down the High Street. This is not a facility that the public wants to see closed. 2013 is its 60th year bringing an anticipated 300 more babies into Stroud.

2006

Brunel 200

The coming of the railway to Stroud in 1845 was fully celebrated in this six month long programme of events and exhibitions joining in the west of England's celebrations of the 200th birth of Brunel and God's Own Railway.

A committee of 10

2007

Cashes Green Hospital Redevelopment

Initiated by Gloucestershire Land for People (Stroud Commonwealth) and now being run by a community land trust, this new development called Applewood comprises 78 new homes. Each home has at least one parking space as well as dedicated bicycle storage. There is a variety of green spaces including a 'pocket orchard' next to the entrance of the project and a natural wildlife corridor that runs through the site from north to south. Homes on the main square have garden gates that open directly onto a generous landscaped square. Applewood is designed by Kevin McCloud's Haboakus company and is being built by Markey's.

Martin Large, Max Comfort

2008

Save Local Post Offices

Stroud Town Council stepped in to save Uplands post office after a concerted campaign from local people and a court case so that the post office did not shut because it was less than a mile from the centre of Stroud.

2006

Transition Stroud

A network for local people (now over 1000 around the world) developing practical answers to the question: How can our community respond to the challenges, and opportunities, of peak oil and climate change? Transition Stroud supports Stroud Food Hub, Edible Open Gardens, Eco Open Gardens, Skills Gain.

2008

The Exchange

Stroud Commonwealth sets up a start-up enterprise centre, The Exchange, on Brick Row fully restored as a energy provider by 2010 with ground source heat pumps and photo voltaic panels. There is hot desking and conference facilities.

Max Comfort

2009

Stroud a Bee Guardian Town

An initial meeting in 2009 discussed the plight of bees. Stroud Town Council pledged not to use pesticides in the town's 24 Green Spaces and to use bee-friendly pollination plants. Stroud became the first bee guardian town. Now the organisers are encouraging Gloucester to become the first bee guardian city.

2009

Allsorts

The name Allsorts seems to capture exactly what it is: allsorts of children, allsorts of grown-ups and most of all allsorts of activities and events. Based in the Stroud Valleys and covering the whole of Gloucestershire, they welcome anyone with a child or young person with additional needs or disabilities, with or without a diagnosis. Together, they develop new activities, working with other organisations to ensure that they can be as effective as they can in supporting not only children with additional needs but also their families.

2010

Stroud Foodbank

To start with it was essential to set up networks for referrals and recruit volunteers. In the first year 900 people were helped and in Year 2, 2000. Now also running Kids Stuff, offering all those necessary items when starting a family.

Will Mansell, Jeremy Nottingham, Brian Oosterhuysen

2011

Stroud Against the Cuts

Initial campaign to stop 3000 county NHS workers being opted out of the NHS into a social enterprise. An injunction stopped the process. New options were offered – set up a Gloucestershire Trust or put the work out to tender. Voting closed mid October with the new trust idea winning hands down.

Chris Moore, James Beecher, Caroline Malloy, John Marjoram

2011

Stroud Community Woodlands

Set up as an industrial and provident society to take on Follywoods with a committee and members who maintain and enjoy Follywoods for all public access.

2012

Stroud Community TV

Over 600 films uploaded all about Stroud – add new films as and when wanted. Through 2012/13 working under Transition Stroud. Offer a monthly newsletter update.

2011/12

GlosVain

Anti incinerator planned for Javelin Park, Haresfield. Argument for – no more landfill and electricity generation. Arguments against – most of the waste needed to keep the incinerator going can be recycled. March 2013 all County Councillors voted against. Next, the developers appeal, November/January 2013/14. If successful the incinerator will be built.

2011/12

Stroud Against the Gyratory

Working on SDC/GCC designs to keep the old Wallbridge open for pedestrians and bicycles and not for cars to give better access into the town.

2012

Stroud Apple Orchards

Funds raised to look after the apple trees planted along the Ebley by Pass and plans to develop more apple growing around the town.

2013

Stroud Against Supermarket Saturation

With potential new supermarkets at Ryeford and the Daniels Estate SASS are working on ways to support more industry and fewer supermarkets and to ensure that local shops in town centres continue to thrive.

Appendix

3

Links, Contacts & References

The links below relate to the organisations written about and referenced through the book. They are divided into local and national contacts. The publications and papers listed are a mix of published and non published texts and have come from personal collections as most are now out of print.

LOCAL CONTACTS

The Old Convent

Beeches Green, Stroud, GL5 4AD, Tel: 01453 757641

Shire Training Workshops/OPENhouse

Tel: 01453 759400

www.openhouse.me.uk

Stroud Preservation Trust

www.stroudpreservationtrust.org.uk

Stroud Valleys Project

8 Threadneedle St, Stroud GL5 1AF, Tel: 01453 753358

www.stroudvalleysproject.org

Stroud Farmers' Market

www.fresh-n-local.co.uk/markets/stroud

Made in Stroud

16 Kendrick Street, Stroud GL5 1AA, Tel: 01453 840265

www.madeinstroud.co.uk

Lansdown Hall and Gallery

Lansdown, Stroud, GL5 1BB, Tel: 01453 767576

www.lansdownhall.org

Transition Stroud

www.transitionstroud.org

The Museum in the Park

Stratford Road, Stroud, GL5 4AF, Tel: 01453 763394

www.museuminthepark.org.uk

Slad Valley Action Group (for Baxter's Fields appeal)

www.savesladvalley.org.uk

Stroud Community TV

www.stroudcommunity.tv

Cashes Green Community Land Trust

www.cashesgreenclt.org.uk

Stroud Valleys Artspace

4 John St, Stroud, GL5 2HA, Tel: 01453 751440

www.sva.org.uk

Stroud District Council

Ebley Mill, Ebley Wharf, Stroud GL5 4UB, Tel:01453 766321

www.stroud.gov.uk

Stroud Town Council

58 London Road, Stroud GL5 2AD, Tel: 01453 762817

www.stroudtown.gov.uk

Stroud News and Journal

6 Lansdown Road, Stroud GL5 1BE, Tel: 01453 769411

www.stroudnewsandjournal.co.uk

Stroud Life

14 Union Street, Stroud GL5 2HE, Tel: 01453 755955

www.stroudlife.co.uk

Stroud Common Wealth

The Exchange, Brick Row, Stroud GL5 1DF, Tel: 01453 762271

www.stroudcommonwealth.org.uk

Flies on the Wall

Tel: 07825 370807

www.jobousfield.co.uk

NATIONAL ORGANISATIONS

United Kingdom Association of Preservation Trusts

www.ukapt.org.uk

Urbed

5th Floor, 10 Little Lever Street, Manchester M1 1HR, Tel: 0161 200 5500

www.urbed.com, info@urbed.coop

Farma (National Farmers Retail and Markets Association)

www.farma.org.uk

Transition Network

www.transitionnetwork.org

Severn Wye Energy Agency

Unit 15 Highnam Business Centre, Highnam, GL2 8DN, Tel: 01452 835060

www.severnwye.org.uk

PUBLICATIONS & PAPERS

Nigel Paterson, *The Vernacular Architecture and Buildings of Stroud and Chalford* (Oxford, 2006)

Tamsin Treverton Jones, *Memories of Stroud* (Stroud, 2005)

Rebecca Price, *A Study into Local Protest in Stroud, 1975 – present* (2012)

Clare Toy, *The Plotter of Gloucester* (Stroud, 1976). '*The people of Stroud stood up and said No, No, No!*'

Stroud Preservation Trust, Rachel Russell, text, *Putting the roof back on* (Stroud, 2012)

Urbed, *Making the Most of the Industrial Heritage of the Stroud Valleys*, June 1986

Appendix

4

Acknowledgements

There are many sources of information that have inspired and helped this book over and above the 31 people interviewed. We would like to acknowledge the following:

The interviewing team

Left to right: Peter Richardson, Camilla Hale, Dominique Shead, Rachel Russell, Hugh Barton and thanks to Steve Barratt

The writing team

Camilla Hale and Dominique Shead

The professional team

Paul Welch for the hours of design and thoughtful support throughout the writing process, *www.welchpix.co.uk*

Dominique Shead, freelance book editor and proofreader, *dshead@btinternet.com*

Steve Hurrell for almost all the biography portraits, *stevehurrell@mac.com*

Training from Beth Whittaker, *www.viva-communications.co.uk*

Jeannette Bond at Bond Secretarial Services for all the audio typing of the interviews, *www.bond-tss.co.uk*

Images

With thanks to all the organisations for generous access to and use of their photographic and press archives

Photographers: Steve Hurrell, John Daniell, Fred Chance

Bill Hicks and Alan Caig for their 'selfie' portraits.

And thanks also to those below who gave help, time, ideas, images and memories

Jo Carrier and Tasha Flaherty at OPENhouse

Eric and Mary Jarrett from RSVP

Other people's interviews from various news articles – John Marjoram, Ron Birch and David Drew in particular.

Peter Waller

Nick Falk from Urbed.

Rachel Russell for her text from the Stroud Preservation Trust brochure, *'Putting the roof back on'* which added enormously to the SPT chapter.

Quotes written by Jo Bousfield, Jonathan Nunn, Tim Harrison, Camilla Hale, Stella Parkes and Anne Mackintosh.

Sarah Parker for the copy of the original Urbed report.

Andrew Wood

PhotoStroud and Kel Portman for ISBN aid

Roger Franklin for always fighting on...

The trustees of Stroud Preservation Trust for their support through this year of celebrating Stroud Preservation Trust's 30th anniversary.

The name of the Community Planning Conference shop located in the centre of Stroud, 1996

Supported by
The National Lottery®
through the Heritage Lottery Fund

heritage
lottery fund

Maps

STROUD DISTRICT LOCATIONS

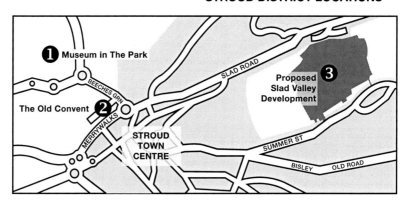

STROUD TOWN CENTRE LOCATIONS

1. OPENhouse/British School
2. Lansdown Hall & Gallery
3. Delmont's Lot
4. Withey's Yard
5. 48 High Street
6. Medieval Hall
7. Stroud Valleys Project
8. Stroud Valleys Arts
9. Farmers' Market

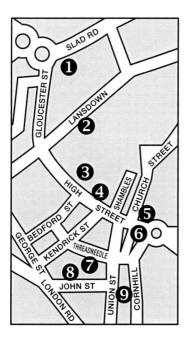